DI HARRIS
STOP DIETING
AND LOSE WEIGHT

This book is dedicated to my past and present clients for sharing their stories and giving me inspiration and encouragement to share my work with others.

Di Harris Seminars is a Registered Business
NO. U9874039

Copyright © Di Harris 1999

This book is not to be reproduced in any way without permission from the publisher. All rights reserved.

First published in 1999

A Di Harris publication
PO Box 359
Blackheath NSW 2785
Australia

National Library of Australia
Cataloguing-in-Publication Data

Harris, Di
Stop Dieting and Lose Weight

ISBN 0-9586031-0-3

1. Weight loss. 2. Self-help. 3. Women's health

Main Editor: Astra Niedra
Sub Editor: Catherine Hammond
Typesetting: J&M Typesetting
Cover and text design: Gayna Murphy
Photographer: Petrina Tinsley
Publisher: Di Harris Seminars
Printer: Australian Print Group
Distributor: Gary Allen Pty Ltd

DISCLAIMER
This book contains the opinions and ideas of the author, Di Harris. These opinions and ideas offer no guarantee of success, nor are they to be taken as professional advice. Readers must accept that they are entirely responsible for any actions they may take as a result of what is written in this book and hold the author free from any responsibility whatsoever for the actions or decisions they may take as a result of reading this book.

DI HARRIS is a renowned speaker and author in the field of self help and weight loss. Di developed her successful formula after a lifetime of unsuccessful dieting left her frustrated and still overweight. After 15 years of research, working with the best in the field, she not only lost weight but developed the most successful program for permanent weight loss, condensed from the best information she discovered. Through her seminars she has helped many women lose weight, regain their normal eating patterns and get back to enjoying life without any hang-ups about, or obsessions with, food or weight. Di's professional training background and her first hand experience have made her a dynamic, fun and passionate speaker and author. She conducts seminars throughout Australia.

ACKNOWLEDGEMENTS

Many people have played a vital part in the success of this book. Personally, I would like to thank my husband Kev (who is thin as a rake and claims "you can't fatten a Thoroughbred") for his keen eye for detail, patience, tolerance and unconditional love. He is simply the best! Thanks to Andrew Griffiths for his patience, perfectionism, enthusiasm and extreme generosity with time; to Michael Rowland for his knowledge, wisdom and guidance and my mother, father, brother and Judi for their love and support.

Professionally I would like to thank:

Firstly, two great ladies who generously gave of their time and talent to get this book up and running; I thank Fiona Schultz for her honesty, guidance and knowledge and Gayna Murphy for her creativity, dedication and help in so many areas.

Thanks also to Astra Niedra my main editor for her skill and expertise to make this book the best it can be, Catherine Hammond for her impeccable line editing and Mike Kuszla for his speed in typesetting this book.

To those early teachers who bought the non-dieting approach to the world and have helped countless women to find happiness and a healthy weight without dieting, I am indebted to: Susie Orbach, Jane R. Hirschmann, Carol H. Munter and Geneen Roth. For first introducing me to this work I thank Penelope Goward.

And finally, to all those friends, family and workshop participants who have encouraged me to continue on this path amongst the highs and the lows, this book, to a large extent, is a result of their belief and support.

Dianne Harris

CONTENTS

Dedication v
Introduction 1

PART ONE
COME OUT OF THE DARK 1
CHAPTER ONE The untold story 3
CHAPTER TWO The real truth behind diets 5
CHAPTER THREE Do you really want to be slim? 13
CHAPTER FOUR Your beliefs hold the key 25
CHAPTER FIVE Become master of your mind 37
CHAPTER SIX Accelerate your progress 43

PART TWO
A NEW BEGINNING 51
CHAPTER SEVEN Check out your eating style 53
CHAPTER EIGHT Awaken your sleeping power 57
CHAPTER NINE Stages on your new journey 59

PART THREE
KISS DIET DRAMAS GOOD BYE 63
CHAPTER TEN So long to sneak eating! 65
CHAPTER ELEVEN Bye bye binge 71
CHAPTER TWELVE Taking the 'guilt' out of food 79

PART FOUR
YOUR STEPS TO SUCCESS 89
CHAPTER THIRTEEN Your body knows best 91
CHAPTER FOURTEEN Your hunger is your best friend 95
CHAPTER FIFTEEN How to eat what you want and enjoy it 105
CHAPTER SIXTEEN Enjoy the abundance and
atmosphere of food 113

CHAPTER SEVENTEEN Knowing when to stop –
mastering satisfaction 119
CHAPTER EIGHTEEN Handling social eating 127

PART FIVE
EMOTIONAL HAPPINESS WITHOUT FOOD 133
CHAPTER NINETEEN How to feel emotions without
needing food 135
CHAPTER TWENTY Activate your power for emotional mastery 143
CHAPTER TWENTY-ONE Personal power comes from
exploring emotions 151

PART SIX
HOW TO LIKE YOUR BEAUTIFUL BODY 159
CHAPTER TWNETY-TWO Thighs, lies and body image 161
CHAPTER TWENTY-THREE How to like the whole package 169
CHAPTER TWENTY-FOUR Clothes size victims 173
CHAPTER TWENTY-FIVE Body movement — the new
approach to exercise 177
CHAPTER TWENTY-SIX How to rapidly increase
your self-esteem 181

PART SEVEN
HOW TO TRAVEL THE HIGHWAY TO SUCCESS 191
CHAPTER TWENTY-SEVEN Planning guarantees success 199
CHAPTER TWENTY-EIGHT Putting it all together 198
CHAPTER TWNETY-NINE Questions and answers 203
CHAPTER THIRTY Where to from here? 207

BIOGRAPHY AND FURTHER READING 211

INTRODUCTION

What you are about to read in this book will liberate you from all unsuccessful weight loss attempts in a way you never dreamed possible. It holds the key to many secrets you must know if you want to lose weight and have a happy relationship with food and your body.

No doubt you have dreamed about living a life at your perfect weight and staying that way. A life of enjoying all kinds of food again with family and friends, with a body that you love.

Well, there is a way which has been hidden from you, a way that is so simple and enjoyable, yet so powerfully effective. The information you will discover is easy to understand and will be easy to apply in your life right now — and you will start to see the benefits immediately.

You are already perfect. The reason you are overweight and unhappy is only because you have been misinformed about the way to permanent weight loss and peace of mind. It isn't a road of hard slog, deprivation and self-hate; it is exciting and full of fun and freedom. I'm here to share my secrets with you of another way to lose weight that is easier and far more healthy, a way that gives you back self-esteem, self-control and happiness. This new way breaks all the rules you have been brought up to believe. It is the way that leads you to your perfect weight, without diets and external control. There are so many other bonuses you will gain along the way: you will learn so much about yourself and your body; you will gain a deep understanding of why you are out of control with food and your weight; and you will be given the secret keys to help you replace all the habits that bring you misery with habits that bring you happiness and self-love. The beauty of this knowledge is that it is designed to enable you to step back into the picture with everyone else and become a happy, normal eater, at the size nature intended you to be.

Your ideal body size is about you as an individual woman who, once she accepts herself and gets in touch with her natural body cycles, will transform into that butterfly she is meant to be. You are embarking on a journey of new discoveries about yourself and your body. Underneath all your frustration, disillusionment and excess weight is your ideal body size wanting to get out and show you the way. I am going to show you how to do just that.

Look at what you will become
From this:
You wake up, your first thoughts are: "What did I eat yesterday that I should not have?" "What should I eat today?" "How can I lose weight more quickly?" "What should I wear to look thin?" You jump on the scales and you let them dictate your mood for the day, depending on which way the needle moves — up means a bad day, down means a good day. You think of food most of the day — what you should and should not eat. You worry about putting on weight and overeating and you feel guilty about what you have just eaten. You never eat high-calorie foods in front of people; you rarely sit down to eat; you eat in secrecy, on the run, in the car, standing at the cupboards or fridge; and you always feel guilty about the amounts and type of food you eat. You compare your figure to others and always want to be thinner. Your weight is a constant roller coaster, never remaining stable, and you are never happy with your body.

To this:
You wake up feeling good, knowing that you don't have a weight problem, physically or mentally. You don't have food or your figure on your mind. You eat what you really feel like. You do not feel guilty eating high-calorie food and you can enjoy eating all foods without guilt. You don't think about food until you are physically hungry. You like to sit down and enjoy food. You can put your knife and fork down between mouthfuls, and you can leave food on the plate. You wear clothes that you like to wear, that make you feel good. You don't count calories or ever weigh yourself. You are at a weight that nature intended you to be at and you love who you are, inside and out.

INTRODUCTION

There is such a dramatic jump between the above two scenarios, isn't there? And achieving this turnaround is nowhere near as hard as sticking to a diet! It *is* within your reach; you don't have to fantasise anymore; reality is just around the corner, in these pages! I and many other women have achieved this turnaround; you can, too.

What you have in these pages is priceless. It is a combination of over fifteen years of research from the very best that is around. Together with my own and other women's personal experiences, it is a book full of true gems. I have taken the best of what I have discovered and put it together into a simple, fun format that will guide you down the correct path to permanent weight loss.

For inspiration, motivation and help, you only have to open these pages. I am here all the time; you can call on me night and day. As you read through these pages you will be delighted at the changes you will make and you will want to include them into your life. You will be surprised how little effort will be required and, as a consequence, you will have more time to enjoy your life.

So get ready to peel away the surface mask and look at the real issues behind your eating. I will show you how to get in touch with your body's natural cycles so that you can lose weight without dieting, be at peace with yourself and get on with enjoying the freedom and fun that life has to offer. I've been there and conquered. I now want to share the experiences and knowledge I have gained by taking this journey of rediscovery — come along with me!

PART ONE

COME OUT OF
THE DARK

CHAPTER ONE

THE UNTOLD STORY

You, dear reader, need to know the real story. You need to know that the dieting era is coming to an end and the simple truth about losing weight can be told to you once and for all, so you can get on with enjoying life. No doubt you have spent many years living 'on hold', waiting to get to your ideal body size before really having a good time. Wait no more! You have all the answers within you. It is just that they have long been buried and squashed by inaccurate beliefs and actions.

What is going to be revealed to you will re-spark your intuition. You will start to feel very excited as you begin to realise how familiar it all seems. The stirring inside you will be busting to get out and show you the path to success that you have known all along.

My job is to re-spark your flame of knowledge and bring the buried secrets to light. I will guide you in their proper usage so you will be guaranteed not just weight loss but a happy and free relationship with food and your body, so that you can regain mastery and power for a great life at the size nature intended you to be.

Take your diet glasses off. They have no place in your life any more. See the world now with fresh, new, perceptive eyes. The first thing you will notice is that the media industry is telling you how you should look and that only when you get this so-called 'look' will you be happy. In the past you would have gone out to get 'the look' and from time to time you may have given the whole game away in disgust, telling yourself you will remain fat and happy and 'stick it up the lot of you'.

The diet industry knows you will try to run away and they have invented methods for capturing you again. New games to play, like 'Don't just diet, count fat grams' and 'Eat what you like — just so long as it's on my menu'. So back you may have gone, to play another round, but now you see through it all. You know the game is up. Deep down you know you have the power and all the answers within you.

CHAPTER TWO

THE REAL TRUTH
BEHIND DIETS

The truth is that diets do not work because they fail to address the real issues of why you are overweight and why you overeat. You only have to look back to how many failed attempts you have had to see that something isn't working.

The diet industry has the best statistics I have seen: a 95 per cent failure rate!
The diet industry has never come up with the correct formula for permanent weight loss. Statistics are proof: 95 per cent of people who go on diets put the weight back on, and usually more, within two years. Diets are only a temporary fix to your weight problem, which is why you have to keep going back on them. All kinds of schemes are there to lure you back, from new 'revolutionary' weight-loss plans, courses, machines, gadgets, bulking agents and replacement meals, to laxatives, diet pills and liquids. The industry knows this and it knows ways to entice you by playing on your weaknesses so that you will come back, time and time again. The media and diet industry feed off each other. One shows you how you should look; the other shows you how to get 'the look'. But these images are totally unrealistic and very

hard work to achieve, which is why they are there — to keep dangling the carrot before you, just out of your reach. The diet industry makes you feel as if *you* are the problem, yet the opposite is true!

The fact is that diets are one of the main reasons you have a weight problem! It's rather ironic, don't you think? Yet why do you still live in a fairytale world of belief that the next diet will be the one that you will stick to effortlessly, causing you to keep the weight off forever, and solving your problems? You skip from diet to diet, trying to find the pot of gold at the end of the rainbow, knowing deep inside that it really does not exist.

We have been conditioned to believe that if we diet and lose weight we will be happy, so when we don't achieve this, we think something is wrong with us and we chop and change diets, spending more and more money in the diet industry, thinking that it is the only path to take and that the fault lies in us.

Why diets don't work
1. Diets are physically impossible to stay on
Can you remember how many diets you have been on throughout your life? Pretty well impossible, isn't it? I remember all my 15 painful years of dieting all too vividly.

The Israeli Army diet was the first diet I embarked on at the age of eleven. I remember marching at school and I fainted — my last thought was "please, no more apples". I joined many weight club groups, one of them sixteen times! I used to go to different clubs as I was too embarrassed going back to the same place more than three times. I hated my scales with a passion. When the needle shifted in the wrong direction, I would be totally devastated, my life in ruins.

An assistant from a weight group I had just joined asked me: "What special occasion would you like to look slim for?" I looked at her rather perplexed, as I wanted to look slim not just for one occasion, I wanted to be slim for them all, for the rest of my life. Needless to say, I never went back. Then came another string of endless diets; you name it, I tried it — and so probably have you, my dear friend. I would shudder to think of all the money we have all spent on diets, clubs and gadgets (you know the type: don't do anything, just lie there and all your fat will be vibrated away — sounds great; no effort, but lots of money). The more desperate I was, the more money I spent.

'Diet' and 'jail' are both four-letter words, and they are very similar in meaning. We get massive hunger sensations from dieting as a result of the restricted food intake — is it any wonder we eat copious amounts of food when we break a diet? And, of course, the stricter the diet, the bigger the binge. Diets set us up for failure as they allow no room for mistakes. It's like someone has said to us: "Oh no, bad girl. Go right back to square one and pay an extra $200.00 while you are there". I have certainly made a few costly mistakes and errors in my time! When we start feeling like a failure we then start eating out of control, and our thoughts are totally focused on the unacceptable shape of our bodies and how quickly we can go on another diet to fix this up. No doubt a picture is being conjured up in your mind of how crazy this all is.

2. Diets make you behave rather neurotically
Once we are told "No, no, no, not allowed", our behaviour takes on a slightly panicky and crazed form. Inner signals register panic, as the warning bells of 'deprivation time coming' ring loud and clear in our heads.

Food and weight obsessed me 90 per cent of the day. I was always thinking about eating or not eating, planning a binge or planning my next diet. I was totally obsessed. My behaviour seemed crazy. I remember the lengths I would go to in order to eat in secrecy, such as hiding food in filing cabinets, wardrobes and under the car seat! It was not a pleasant or empowering way to live, but so many of us live like this, completely obsessed with weight and food issues, our beliefs so ingrained that we can see no way out. I never was able to imagine a life free of food obsessions and weight worries.

Only now can I look back and see the funny side to many eating episodes. I can laugh at all those times on the way home from work when I stopped off at the shop and bought lollies, chips, ice-creams — 'just for the kids' — only to polish the lot off before I arrived home, all evidence carefully and with criminal precision taken care of. Or the times I threw out food that was considered 'bad' in the bin, only to dig it out later and finish it off. I can see you smiling at these situations — perhaps they are familiar to you, too. Don't feel embarrassed, we all have a few funny stories to tell. At the time when these eating episodes took place, I didn't see the funny side. I felt embarrassed, silly, fat and out of control.

3. Diets turn normal eaters into people who fear food
Dieter's belief: Start diet Monday, stuff face Sunday.
Being stuck in diet mentality blocks our clear thinking, and what results are actions which hinder weight loss and increase our obsessions. What happens when you think 'diet'? I think 'food', 'stuff as much in as I can before D-day' (which is usually Monday). So on Sunday evening you have a bit of a feast. In goes the food. But it's not just any old food. It has to be the forbidden type: chocolate, biscuits, cakes, chips, ice cream. You name it, in it goes, so long as it's fattening. The name of the game is 'fit in as much as you can'. I used to always think that if only I could feel this full for the rest of my dieting days, I wouldn't have any problem sticking to a diet! Alas, that thought couldn't be further from the truth.

We play this diet game as we have convinced ourselves that the last meal before the diet is the last chance we'll get to eat the foods we crave, the ones that we forbid ourselves to eat. It really is the feast before the famine. As soon as you tell yourself you can't have a particular food, the desire to have it increases 300 per cent. This is human nature, so do not try to fight it!

Following is an extract from my personal diary. You may find some similarities to your own 'diet Mondays'!

> "7.00 am: I wake up feeling determined that this diet is the magical one that will work. I will lose 10 kg in 2

months. My willpower is so strong, I will not weaken or fail. I weigh myself — oh dear, more than I thought. I move the scales around for the best weight reading, but it's still not good. I religiously prepare breakfast:
* 'No-added-sugar' orange juice
* 1 toast with low-fat margarine and jam
* Coffee, skim milk (ugh)

7.30 am: I eat. I really want a croissant now more than I ever did.

8.15 am: I'm on my way to work. All I see is thin women and fattening food. I believe they have all come out of the woodwork to test me. Some of these women are eating food in front of me. Damn cheek, they know I am on a diet and are doing it just to spite me. I feel like ramming the food down their skinny, scrawny necks! How can she eat that and be so slim?

9.00 am: Walking to the office, all the forbidden foods are jumping out at me. Chocolate bars nearly hit me on the head and cakes at the bakery are talking to me. I put it all aside, and with grim determination I trudge on. I am so sick of being totally obsessed with food. I can't get into my work, every thought break and its food, food, food. When am I next going to eat? Oh gosh, its only 10.30 am! 12 noon comes around and I'm a hungry beast. A cold salad and dry biscuits is the last thing in the world I want. I eat, then something snaps and I just go into a frenzy. I buy chocolates, chips. All I can think about is stuffing it down as quickly as I can without anyone seeing me.

Dieter's belief: I've eaten one bit of 'bad' food, so I may as well go the whole way.

5.30 pm: I drive the long way home, stopping off at a grocery shop where they don't know me. "They are for the kids", I say. I eat and stuff my face. Stopping at the traffic lights is no real issue. Other drivers only see my face and not my large body.

6.30 pm: I get home, I eat in the toilet and flush at the same time so Kev can't here the noise of the opening of lolly papers. (Don't you just hate noisy wrappers? I'm sure they wrap lollies in them just to annoy us diet-breakers). I feel like a criminal. It's like the Dr Jekyll-Mr Hyde syndrome. One minute I am normal, the next I'm a slobbering wide-eyed maniac. (Have you ever seen yourself in the mirror at this point? Look sometime, it's worth a laugh)."

4. Diets make you feel guilty and rebellious
"Then the guilt sets in. Oh the shame, the guilt, the physical pain of eating too much. I look in the mirror and appear twice the size I was this morning. I really believe I have put on 3 kilos in one day. I see a few pimples — that just tops it off. After the binge, the guilt and depression set in. I go on my downward spiral for weeks, in and out of bingeing, waiting for the day I can muster up the courage to go on another diet."

I'm sure the above story is familiar to all of you and it clearly illustrates what a lot of unnecessary pain we put ourselves through to lose weight through diet mentality. Our actions go totally against our natural instincts. We completely surrender our power to an external force and, on a subconscious level, this makes us very angry, guilty and obsessive. How absurd it really is to let some unknown authority tell us when to eat, what to eat and how much we should eat. No wonder we become slightly neurotic and obsessive.

Being deprived of our most basic pleasure in life causes us to feel quite rebellious and deprived, to say the least. How many of you can remember a wedding or social function where you showed so much self-control by not eating all the goodies, only to feel so terribly deprived once you got home? Once home you feel angry at denying yourself all those goodies and you fill yourself up by eating a few miserable goodies that are in your fridge and cupboards, cursing yourself for not just 'pigging out' on all those treats when you had the chance.

What makes us act like this? Feeling that food is our enemy and using our body as the battleground?

The answer lies in finding and understanding and working with, not against, the perfect body that nature has given you. Right now you may be thinking this is a bit of a joke, as you look in the mirror, but let's face it: five, ten, twenty, thirty or more years of desperately trying to lose weight through dieting and strict exercise hasn't helped you, has it? You know the overall effects of losing and putting on weight are far worse than being constantly overweight. All that emotional pressure and the physical pressure of going from one extreme to another eventually takes its toll.

Making the break
Get off the Mad Mouse Wheel

Our lives are like the mouse who keeps going on his wheel, never getting anywhere, not realising that the solution lies in getting off the wheel. You must get off this wheel of madness and the only way to do that is to first give up dieting and food restricting, for it serves no purpose.

Mad Mouse Wheel

How does giving up diets forever make you feel? Does it make you feel anxious that you have no external watchdog keeping track of you? Does it make you feel ecstatic and free from a lot of misery? Common responses are a mixture of both happy and scared. Most women feel happy that there is a way out of the diet jail, but scared that they may not be able to lose weight without dieting. It is normal to feel scared.

Dieting is like being in jail. You are not taught to think, you are surrounded by four walls and you have no control. Set free, you wouldn't know what to do. The first thing you probably will do is go totally out of control and you may even put on weight! There have been studies done on athletes who lose weight to 'get definition' before competition. Athletes go through feelings of deprivation, like dieters. Once they know they do not have to diet so strictly again, they go on an almighty binge. And after they register that all food is freely available again, they go back to their 'normal' eating patterns.

We have embedded in our minds that dieting is the only way to lose weight. Remember, your body has its own ideal body weight that it is happiest at. Through normal eating patterns your body will return to this size. You may not be a size 10 again, but you must accept your general body shape.

HANDY HINTS

GET OFF THE CYCLE OF DIETING AND BINGEING.

START LOOKING AT YOUR BELIEFS ABOUT EATING/FOOD, AND CHANGE THEM.

GIVE UP DIETING; THIS WILL REDUCE YOUR OBSESSION WITH FOOD.

CHAPTER THREE

DO YOU REALLY WANT
TO BE SLIM???

Dieter's belief: Being slim always seems out of my range.

We have all experienced the pains of dieting and trying to be slim, but do you really want to be slim? Silly question! Of course you want to be slim — but do you really? Your words might say you do, but your thoughts and actions may say something exactly opposite. Hard to believe? Not really, if you understand how your mind works. In fact, you will be quite shocked to find that there are many reasons why you don't want to be slim; and what is more, you probably don't even know they exist!

In our conscious mind we abhor the very thought of being fat. It causes us pain and grief, like feeling ashamed for taking up too much space, being constantly embarrassed, hiding from cameras and refusing invites to the beach or parties. When I was overweight, social gatherings used to be a real trial. One particular Christmas party with a group of friends and relatives I hadn't seen for a while sticks quite clearly in my mind. I had stacked on the weight and no matter how hard I tried, I still hadn't lost any weight. As the day of the party came closer, I abandoned all hope of losing weight. I then tried to think up some great excuse that would get me off the hook. However, so many people were looking forward to seeing me, and Kev was looking forward to going, so I couldn't back out. I spent the last week trying on many different outfits in hope of finding one that would hide my fat the best. I opted for a black jacket and long black skirt (this seems to be the uniform for those of us trying to hide weight gain!).

I didn't feel comfortable at all at the party. Because I felt frumpy and old-fashioned in my outfit, I had stacked on the makeup and tried to make the most of my hair. Not wanting to be hugged too much or converse too much, I hovered in the background and let people approach me. I was eyeing off all the beautiful food but felt too embarrassed to eat, in case people saw me and noticed my weight gain and made silent judgments. I had a thoroughly miserable time, eyeing off with scorn and jealousy my friends and relatives who had lost weight and seeing if they had aged more to compensate for my feeling lousy. Most of the women wore short skirts, which added to my feelings of isolation. My thoughts were so purely self-indulgent misery at being so fat that I forgot to enjoy myself — or, more to the point, I didn't want to enjoy myself and didn't think I was allowed to enjoy myself, being the weight I was. Does this type of story sound familiar to you?

Summertime is another nightmare when we are overweight. Summer means sleeveless dresses, shorts, bathers and revealing clothes to show how overweight we are. At least in winter we can hide the body parts we feel embarrassed about! How many times do you knock back a visit to the beach or river because the pain of your 'fat feelings' is just too great? It is sad to think how many opportunities we miss, or occasions we are miserable at, because we are too engrossed in our misery at being overweight. I am sure you can think of many other situations.

Being 'fat' in our 'thin-obsessed' society is a tough job, and it is hard to understand why we have an interest in staying overweight. The truth is that underlying everything, you do have an interest in being overweight. This interest is largely unconscious, but once you recognise that you have an interest in remaining overweight, you can explore it further and find out whether being big is supposed to do what you want it to do.

Wanting to be thin but needing food to relieve our emotional problems can create a real push-pull situation in our lives. Overeating and being overweight are responses to life's stresses, but they are seldom the best choices and never the only choice we can make. We must first understand the real issues of why we turn to food. This is what we are addressing: the situations in our life that are at the root of it all. Food is just the mask we hide behind.

If you are to give up overeating and explore your issues without turning to food and hiding behind your weight, then you are going to stabilise at a lower weight. For you to feel comfortable with this new constant weight and, more importantly, being a smaller size, you need to understand what your previous interests in being overweight and being preoccupied with food intake mean. If you understand how being large has helped you then you can begin to give it up as you find new ways to help yourself. Before you can really be committed to losing weight for good, you must look at how being overweight serves you. Let's begin by looking more closely at the benefits of overeating and remaining overweight.

Benefits of being overweight
Being 'fat' means I can still keep eating to cope
Picture this scene: you come home after a hard day's work. The house is dirty, the children are fighting and all you want is peace and quiet. You send the children off to play outside and you turn to the fridge. Chocolate bars that you vowed you would not eat stare at you. You start eating the chocolate. In that instant the food tastes delicious. You know it is always there if you want more; it doesn't talk back to you or argue; it doesn't judge you in any way; it won't run away; and it will always give you a quick fix and numb the pain or take away the feelings of anxiousness. The chocolate satisfies your frustrations and soothes your temper, *but only in that instant* and at a huge cost to you. As soon as the instant of the quick fix disappears, you immediately feel that food makes you feel fat, ugly, depressed and disgusting.

With this intimate relationship with food, and with locking our feelings away with it, we will always remain overweight. Most of us are not taught to deal with stress in a constructive way and we find other quick-fix ways to cope, regardless of whether they help or hinder us. As with food, these other quick-fix methods become our medicine for life's stresses.

There was a point in life when you started using food as a coping mechanism. Only now food has become a habit for emotional support. We tend to forget (or may not even be aware) that this is the fact of the situation. It is not the food per se, it is why we brought it into our lives that must be examined.

We have a cozy relationship in our lives with food, ourselves and our problems. We have integrated these three things into our lives, and the dynamic has become too difficult to change.

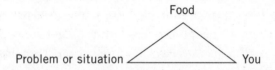

If you take the food out of your life, what will you be left with? Problems and you — you and the original problems or situations that turned you to food in the first place. Life without food is a hard road to travel, as food was the very thing that helped you cope with situations and problems. So when you take food out of your life, you not only deprive yourself of physical satisfaction but you cut out your means for emotional satisfaction. Hence, a very hard dieting phase will follow and soon a binge will result, as you cannot cope without your coping crutch — food. Can you begin to see the picture? It's not as crazy as it seems when we step back and look at it logically and without emotion.

My 'fat' is my only problem
One problem, one solution — let's bury our head in the sand and ignore all the other issues! I know that what I'm suggesting means we lose the false hope that weight loss is the solution to our problem, for it is easier to blame fat for all our problems: "I can't do that, I'm too fat", "I'm not going out socially because I'm too

fat", "They won't want to talk to me because I'm too fat". This list is endless.

Your weight problem is not isolated from the rest of your life, it is part of it. Your weight, body image, relationship happiness, sexual satisfaction, self-esteem are all linked in with your thoughts on food. Any change in your weight effects all these areas of your life and your life's problems influence your weight. I used to always put on weight when I was faced with a challenge, such as having to speak to a group of people or state an opinion — the fear of losing out was so strong. I would turn to food instantly to stop those scary emotions that I didn't want to deal with and didn't know how to deal with. Ahhh ... food was always there as my friend ... and then as my enemy.

We live our lives away, wishing to be thin and if we get thin, we still think we are fat anyway. We put the weight back on and our blame list continues: "It's no use, I have no willpower, maybe I am destined to stay fat". In that instant of the eating act nothing else matters, we can blame all our problems on fat because that is easier to deal with. One problem: fat. One solution: diet. It's easier to remain fat.

I can hide behind my fat
Let's recall my disastrous Christmas party and think of one of your own social situations where you felt the same. As miserable as you may have felt, your fat hid you, protected you. It is like a protective coat, a buffer zone to the world. When we are fat we can hide. Yes, it means we don't have to talk to people, we don't have to be the life of the party, we don't have to be the centre of attention, we don't have to be attractive to men, we don't have to compete with other women. It's safer to remain fat.

Being fat means I don't have to be sexual
Some of us find that when we put on weight, our partners don't make as many sexual advances. Because we are not feeling sexual this affects how our partners feel about us sexually. Some of us like it that way. It's safer to be fat.

Being fat means I won't be admired for my flesh
Many of us are sick and tired of this flesh infatuation. Only when we are overweight can we be taken seriously and talk more intelligently to men. Their minds then will not be doting on our figure. It's safer to be fat.

Being fat means I don't have to worry about sexual advances
A large number of women think it's great not being part of the 'pick-up stakes' and having to worry about competing. Who knows what might happen if we were thin? — all that long-lost attention; we might not be able to control ourselves. It's safer to be fat.

Being fat provides space and protection, a nice buffer zone
Some women liken their fat to a buffer zone. It keeps people at a distance and it means they don't have to get too close — flesh and bone are so exposing. It's safer to be fat.

Being fat means I don't have to compete — no fear of failure
Some of us like this idea. It's nice and comfortable. Letting the pretty, slim women get the boys and the promotions means that we can be safe and we don't have to get involved. It's safer to be fat.

Being fat means I don't have to be perfect
A line I hear a lot is: "Being fat means I can stay with the fantasy of getting a perfect body and a perfect life. Thinking about this fantasy makes my life worth living and makes it worth striving for a happy ending." Sometimes the social expectations of being a woman and being thin are too much for us to handle. On one hand, we need to look good, and on another, we need to be competent wives, mothers and house-runners. It's easier to stay fat.

My husband likes me overweight
Many husbands also like their wives to stay fat. They feel safer thinking that their wives won't stray and that other men won't look at them when they are fat. I have known many cases where

women lose weight and it results in extreme marital jealousy and in some cases divorce. Sue, a workshop participant, said, "I tried to lose weight and when it was quite noticeable Tom would get into rages of jealousy and start feeding me sweets, saying he loved me the way I used to be. To save our marriage from problems, I put the weight back on."

There is individuality in being fat — my fat says "up yours!"; I am who I am
To many of us our current size gives us the freedom to be who we are, to express our personality. Another one of my workshop participants, Karen, said that it was hard for her to picture being thin because she was the family carer, the problem solver, and everyone used to say, "Go to Karen, she is soft and cuddly and you will feel safe in her arms". How could they possibly do that if she were a bag of bones? Karen worked through her issues and settled for a slightly higher ideal weight — one that she could still be cuddly with. She is now at that body size and happy with her new, slimmer, cuddly shape.

Likewise, Lisa was always the life of the party — big and boisterous. She liked it that way and couldn't imagine a slim boisterous Lisa being the life of the party. Lisa remained overweight for quite some time and then she finally broke through and realised she didn't really like being the life of the party. Her deeply ingrained belief was, "If I stay fat I have to compensate in some way". Hence, being the life of the party was the compensating behaviour she developed. Lisa gave up parties and took up studying something which she truly wanted to do and is now moving steadily towards her ideal body shape.

Did a few of these scenarios ring a bell with you? I'm sure they did. Accept that there is truth there; accept the fact that your weight helps you. You must do this if you want to change and get long-term results. Don't think accepting them will keep you remaining overweight — the exact opposite is true. Going deeper and exploring the unconscious benefits to you of remaining overweight will give you the key to change.

Overeating and staying big aren't going to make any of these issues change or go away. It may cover them for a while as our fat provides something less threatening to worry about. You will slowly learn to express yourself directly and not hide from yourself and life with food. Slowly you will start to change as it becomes reassuring to know that you are not destroying yourself with food. This insight provides you with the awareness of what is going on inside you.

Slowly, over time, and with observation, you will be able to see more positive aspects of being overweight. Your image of fat will not be so negative and one-sided. Instead of regarding yourself as a pathetic, hopeless and destructive fat blob, you will be able to see that your eating and your weight have a purpose and serve a function. As this function comes to light you will find that you will not be so hard on yourself. You will start to view your eating and your weight as a way in which you have handled some of life's situations.

Thin ... what does it really mean to you?

If being overweight helps us in a protective way, then being thin can be a fearful state. Quite often we are exposed to the very things we tried to avoid by being fat in the first place. The negatives of being thin are largely unconscious, just like the positives of being fat. Being thin for many of us is usually so far removed from reality it seems like just a fantasy. Fantasies are safe because there is no room for failure — we can always dream and live in hope. If by some miracle we get thin, it is usually not what we thought it would be like, as all our unsolved problems and issues still get lugged with us and we return to our old shape to cope, as that is the only safe way we know.

What do you associate thin and fat with?

When I am thin I would be, have, do ...
When I am fat I can be, do, have ...

Do you get two totally different pictures? Many women conjure up in their minds that being thin means being sexy, on show, perfect, looked at, faultless, and deep inside they think, "Hey, I can't possibly be all of these; it's safer and easier to remain fat, where there is room for all my faults". Let's take a closer look at some of these beliefs.

Thin means being promiscuous
Many of us think thin is sexy, thin is desirable, the lust of all men, the envy of all women. I used to always feel very sexually attractive when I lost weight and the wolf whistles and 'come ons' were real ego boosters. I couldn't for the life of me think why I would want to stack the weight back on! But subconsciously I was in a panic that I might not be able to stop or refuse an advance and I would be unfaithful! It's better to remain fat and faithful.

Being thin means having to be perfect
This is a huge demand to place on yourself, especially with all the other expectations you have of yourself.

Being thin means being a bitch
This thought is in direct conflict with the role we believe that women should play. We believe that as women we should be caring, loving and thoughtful, putting family ahead of ourselves. Thin means being selfish, uncaring, cold and heartless.

Being thin means being in the competition
Competition between women is fierce and painful, even when acted out on an unconscious level. It makes us judge others so we can determine how comfortable we feel. "She is fatter and uglier than me" means that I can feel comfortable. "She is thinner and prettier than me" means that I need to feel uncomfortable. Many of us attempt to avoid these situations and feelings by getting fat. Thinking thin triggers off competition thoughts and sometimes we don't know how we will cope with our judgments.

There are so many reasons for us to put the weight back on, that the 'when I lose weight all my problems will be solved' scenario is translated into 'I am scared and afraid of facing certain issues in my life'. Weight often becomes the convenient scapegoat for other problems in our lives. If we truly want to lead a better life and be kind to ourselves, then the benefits of losing weight must be transformed in our minds. We must detach ourselves from the fear and negativity that we have associated with different body states. This way we can start to express ourselves without any regard to our size. More constructive reasons to lose weight are to increase self-image, increase confidence, enjoy your body more, to have a healthy body, to improve relationships, to allow people to get closer.

This approach to weight loss is one of self-love and a willingness to explore the parts of you that hinder self-growth. It takes courage and commitment but the benefits you gain will be enormous.

Losing weight for the right reasons will give you a much better chance for permanent weight loss. All your issues can be and must be worked on now. Do not put them off until you lose weight — you will never get there! The subconscious saboteur will attack your mind and keep you overweight through fear. Working on your issues now will mean that the psychological benefits will occur before weight loss, and that is a great feeling. It means living in the present and accepting who you are now. This will put you in the right frame of mind for when you lose weight. Working on your issues now means that when you lose your excess weight, you will have also lost all the emotional baggage along the way that prevented you from keeping the weight off in the past.

Making your ideal body weight a reality
It is important that you start now while you are overweight to work on all your issues; otherwise, when you reach your ideal body weight you will not be adapted to your new weight and you will revert back to being fat. You must detach your emotional state from your body weight if you are to succeed at remaining at your new weight.

DO YOU REALLY WANT TO BE SLIM???

Where do you want to be? What body size do you want to be? Based on your lifestyle, age and genetics, is this achievable and attainable? Are you willing to change your eating patterns?

Explore your answers and put time and energy into this change.

Now I want you to close your eyes for two minutes and bring the vision of the new you into focus. With the new you in front of you, melt into your image, breathe deeply and really feel yourself in your mind's image. Do you feel happy, full of vitality, healthy? Can you see yourself eating, talking and doing daily activities? Now open your eyes. If your new vision infused you with good feelings, then this is the ideal body size for you. It doesn't have to be a media-promoted or socially accepted size; it can be any size, as long as it feels right for you. Negative feelings and images will hinder your change; positive feelings will promote faster and lasting change.

HANDY HINTS

Work on your issues NOW, not when you get thin.
Explore the benefits to you of maintaining excess weight and start working on those issues.
Make sure you lose weight for the right reasons.

CHAPTER FOUR

YOUR BELIEFS HOLD
THE KEY

Up until now your food intake is what you have been focusing all your attention on, but has this approach helped you in your weight loss endeavours? No, it has only made you more nutritionally knowledgeable and most likely totally obsessed and still overweight. You need to go one step further than food and that is to explore your *beliefs* about food.

Your thoughts and beliefs about food play a big part in why you have a weight problem. Let's have a good think about that statement. "How can my beliefs keep me fat?" I hear you ask. Well, how many times have you said things like, "Oh, I only have to look at a piece of cake and I gain three kilos" or "I couldn't possibly eat one piece of chocolate — no, if I am going to eat it I have to eat it all" or "I have no willpower, it is useless, I like food too much so it looks like I'm destined to stay fat"? The list goes on and on. You see, what you tell yourself is how you will end up acting — thinking you can't stop at one bite guarantees you won't!

Where do your thoughts come from?
You may think that your thoughts come from your conscious mind, but your conscious mind contains only a small percentage

of them. The vast majority of your thoughts, beliefs and knowledge are housed in your subconscious mind and are the driving force behind all your actions. The thoughts that come into your mind must come from somewhere within you, and they can only come from what has already been implanted into your subconscious mind. These thoughts and beliefs come from life's experiences, our families, friends, school teachers, TV, radio, media and our culture. Everything in your life is stored in your memory banks; nothing is ever forgotten. That is why therapies such as rebirthing are so popular, as you can recall any thought when you are in a calm state. Quite amazing things can come to light.

Most people are totally unaware of what is ruling their lives. They think it is external influences that have power over them, yet the exact opposite is true — you are totally responsible for everything that happens to you. Your excess weight and eating problems are there because of your belief structure. Changing the thoughts embedded in your subconscious mind is the key to your success. It is like pulling the weed out, roots and all, whereas just changing what is in your conscious mind is like cutting the weed off at ground level — not effective at all, for the weed will grow back.

Weeds must be pulled out regularly and properly or they will overgrow a garden very quickly. So it is with your mind: old beliefs must be changed in your subconscious mind regularly and your mind must have something new to work with, or it will just keep bringing up the same old weeds when you yearn for roses!

Your beliefs are the key to change

Your body always obeys the instructions of your mind. Think of a very simple activity like making a cup of tea. First you think about having a cup of tea, then you go and make one and drink it. You then think that a biscuit or two would be nice, so you eat them. Then you think, "Oh, this is terrible, I really shouldn't have eaten those biscuits. I can't control myself around food, I can't stop eating these biscuits." Lo and behold, you don't stop, you keep eating and soon all the biscuits are gone and you think, "What a pig I am! I have no control", and that is exactly the way you act.

It is not what you eat that can hurt you, it is what you think and believe about food and yourself that hurts you. Food by itself is not fattening; it is the thoughts/beliefs you have about food and yourself that are the problem. For many years now you have input a belief system that keeps you overweight. For example, if you keep telling yourself you are fat and unattractive, your mind will obey this statement and say, "Okay, if we are going to be fat and unattractive, we must make sure that we will be so". And all your efforts for weight loss will be sabotaged. To top it off, you will also always feel unattractive. The only diet you should be on is a diet to restrict negative thoughts and beliefs and to increase positive thoughts and improve your self-image.

Most common belief about weight loss that prevents success
'Losing weight is too hard'
Of course it is when you consider the only ways that we have been taught how to lose weight: diets, food deprivation, sweating it out at the gym. This is all too much work. When we only have those experiences to focus on, no wonder we say to ourselves, "Staying slim isn't worth the effort, I'd rather keep eating chocolate".

We don't have to give up our small pleasures in life. The key is finding a balance between eating for physical hunger, eating what you want and satisfying emotional hungers in better ways.

What are your thoughts when you wake up in the morning or when you go to bed at night? What are you telling yourself? I'm sure you're not telling yourself how wonderful and lovable and great you are!

Does your diet vocabulary sound like the following? Add more of your own expressions to the list.

"I can't stop at one, I have to eat the lot."
"Weight loss is so difficult — I hate restricting my food."
"I love food too much to give it up."
"Food is bad — it controls me."

"Good foods are low calorie."
"Food is fattening."
"I wish I didn't like food so much."
"If I see food I eat it."
"Losing weight is hard and a constant struggle."
"I have to diet severely to lose weight."
"I must count calories."
"I must weigh myself."

Take a good look at your list — it tells you what your beliefs are. It is your beliefs which prevent you from ever successfully losing weight and enjoying food and your body. Your beliefs have been formed over many years and you constantly reinforce them with your failed weight loss attempts. So to win the losing game, you will need to implant a whole new set of beliefs.

Now do an exercise where you replace your diet beliefs with a new set of beliefs. For example:

Old dieter's belief: My family are all fat; I am destined for the same future.

New belief: I have courage to break this pattern; weight loss is entirely up to me.

A good way to start implementing your new beliefs is to focus on one or two that you really want to bring into your life. Write them down on a small card and put the card either in your wallet, or on the fridge, or on the mirror — anywhere you look frequently. The aim is to pick yourself up and start repeating your new beliefs as frequently as you can, every day, until they are firmly embedded into your subconscious. Before you wake up and go to sleep, repeat them to yourself and visualise yourself in this new mind-set.

The real power behind your thoughts

Let's take a look at a typical eating episode and see how powerful our thoughts really are.

Scene To eat or not to eat
BELIEF/THOUGHT: I have been so good with my eating this week. I haven't had any sugar; I deserve a treat. Those chocolate

biscuits look so delicious, I'm drooling. But if I have one, I've blown it. I can't stop at one, I always end up going on a feeding frenzy. They will just be the tip of the iceberg.

ACTION: You eat two chocolate biscuits and then you say: "How stupid was that! I shouldn't have done that. I've blown it now. I've got no willpower. My eating is totally out of control. I will never be able to lose weight. I always fail.

FEELINGS: Guilt, sadness, depression, fear of being out of control, fear of future deprivation.

BEHAVIOUR: You take a third and fourth biscuit and, before you know it, you have gobbled down the whole packet and have started on other food. You collapse on the chair, stuffed and miserable, and fall asleep.

Your beliefs are your spoken word

Listen and pay attention to your spoken words and the self-talk inside your head. Sit quietly for five minutes and observe your self-talk. How much of it is positive? How many times do you say 'I should', 'I ought', 'I must'? These words make your life like a jail, where you live by harsh rules and beliefs. Other words that cause a great deal of unhappiness are 'must' and 'have'. 'I must be slim', 'I have to lose weight' — these expressions bring with them feelings of desperation and panic. Change these words to 'choose': 'I choose to be slim' sounds a lot better; there is no desperation and it sounds more powerful and in control. 'Don't' is another word that will not help you change at all. If you say to yourself 'don't eat that', your mind will forget the 'don't' and pick up on the 'eat that'. Change 'don't' into words that have a better outcome. For example, change 'I don't want to eat anything that makes my tummy bloated' to 'I choose not to eat anything that makes my tummy bloated' — this statement sounds less harsh and more self-empowering.

Start to fill your head with positive self-talk in the morning, just before you get out of bed, and in the evening, before you go to bed. You can write yourself a positive letter, such as the following:

"Dear ... I think you are great. You are a wonderful,

loving and beautiful person. I will follow my new intuitive way to eating to the best of my ability and any setback I will treat as a learning experience. I will always treat myself with love and kindness."

Your mind opens up more in the morning and evening as you are still in the subconscious realm, so doing these exercises at these times will enable the new thoughts to sink in deeper, having more impact on your actions.

Believing other people's words

If someone told you that you were fat, that you will never lose weight because you have no willpower or self control, would you turn around and say "No, you are wrong; I can change anything in my life"? Hardly. Most of the time we believe what people say and let these words rule and ruin our lives. These words go into our subconscious mind and sabotage any attempts at weight loss.

What words have you been told that have stuck? For example: "You have the frame to stay large", "All our family have always been big", "You have a slow metabolism". If these beliefs are deeply ingrained and not disposed of, they will sabotage any effort at weight loss.

Believing the media

Television addiction queens are everywhere. I changed the day of my workshops from a Tuesday to Wednesday evening because all my would-be participants were at home glued to *Melrose Place*! What messages does that show send out? Being a bitch, slim and beautiful gets you what you want? Although you know it isn't reality, your subconscious mind does not know this, and all the information gets filtered into the deep layers of your mind. There are hundreds of other shows and magazines that speak the same sentiments. They are everywhere, at the supermarket checkout, plastered over the windows of news agencies, all spewing out utter garbage. Who really cares if Elizabeth Taylor hasn't had a facelift or Demi Moore shaves her head? I personally have more important things on my agenda. Be very careful what you feed your mind, as the information you feed it will help or hinder your growth.

So much of our media is filled with garbage that turns us into gossip addicts and women who are paranoid about our body, age and beauty. What you read, watch on television and listen to becomes your life. I stopped watching the news, reading women's magazines and going to self-obsessed gym groups because they all had a negative effect on me. Start paying very close attention to what fills up your life. Make sure it is quality, and don't stand for anything that makes you feel lousy. Remember, all the messages you take in from your external world make their way into your subconscious mind. Your subconscious mind takes everything literally; it can't distinguish fact from fiction.

What shows do you watch on television? What magazines do you read? What is the general theme of conversation you have with friends? How much of your time per day is spent on these activities? Do these activities help or hinder your growth?

The steps to change your thoughts
1. Visualisation (seeing your new belief)
There is nothing your mind loves more than images. Their power is phenomenal. Great masters and athletes visualise themselves succeeding or winning before a big event.

The key to effective visualisation is that the image you visualise must be fuelled with passion and faith and it needs to be visualised for five minutes, once a day, for a minimum of two months.

Stop daydreaming that 'when you are thin, you will enjoy life' and start putting your images to good use.

Technique:
Spend a few minutes relaxing and deep breathing and feeling happy. Spend five minutes visualising the body shape you want now, in the present. Really see and feel your new shape. See yourself eating and enjoying a variety of food, joining in with friends and family. See yourself leaving food on your plate, feeling

satisfied and not over-full. Feel the power and freedom you get from being in control. Really breathe in the wonderful emotions as you play this scene in your mind. Your mind is an open canvas, so only paint the best pictures on it. If negative thoughts enter your mind, open your eyes, breathe them out and then continue.

Do you feel like you are really there? Add positive and happy emotions into your scene and make sure, in your mind, that you reach or have what it is you desire.

2. Affirmations: thinking and writing your new beliefs

Affirmations enhance visualisation and help reprogram the old beliefs in your subconscious mind. Affirmations are short positive statements that are simple and easy to understand. Affirmations work on filling your mind with thoughts that support what you want to achieve. Affirmations should be written or spoken at least twenty times per day for a minimum of two months for them to be of any benefit. I use them everywhere — in my car, on my bike, out walking, cleaning my teeth, in the shower and, yes, even in the toilet. I will share with you some of my current affirmations:

- I am always full of health and vitality.
- I trust and flow with the process of life.
- Abundance and good things always come to me.

Say your affirmations aloud while looking in the mirror. Write them down and visualise them. Start acting as though you have what you desire. For example, if you are waiting till you get thin to enjoy your life, start doing things you enjoy now. Don't wait; live for now!

If you don't believe you can achieve your affirmations, this is an indication that you feel you are unworthy or don't deserve what you're affirming. Start then with an affirmation of 'I deserve' or 'I love myself' or 'I am a worthwhile, lovable person'. These are your affirmation foundations to build on. Write yourself some affirmations that are positive and that counteract the negatives. For example, counteract the thought 'I am hopeless' with 'I am unique'; 'I hate myself' with 'I accept myself'; and 'I hate all thin women' with 'I am responsible for my own self-image'.

YOUR BELIEFS HOLD THE KEY

Work on your harmful beliefs by first writing down all the negative beliefs you have about yourself. Challenge them and replace them with positive beliefs.

Affirmations are like a seed that is planted. They need constant daily watering and time to grow. You cannot be slim, healthy and happy overnight. Singing your affirmation helps keep it embedded, too. Remember all those ghastly advert jingles that keep playing around in your mind? If you have one floating around, attach your affirmation to it. End your affirmation with 'this or something better now manifests in me'. Shakti Gawain's *Creative Visualisation* is a great book for understanding and working with the power of affirmations.

Many women set off enthusiastically with affirmations but, after a while, self-doubt creeps in and self-talk changes to something along the lines of 'they don't really work' or 'affirmations, they are hopeless'. This negativity is understandable: for ten, twenty or thirty years you have been told that you are fat and have no control. This conditioning will take a while to counter. Treat negativity as a friend who's reminding you that you are now changing. Don't listen to other people's negativity either — that is just giving away your power. Silence is good; it keeps the power within you. Not everything will turn out exactly as you want. Have faith and trust the process of life to give you what is best for you.

Thoughts are very powerful and any image held in your mind will eventually produce some effect. When you change your thoughts/beliefs, your new reality will not follow immediately. There will always be a time lag in which you will be in a position of developing the new you but still stuck in your old world. This 'waiting to happen' phase is important because, if you react positively, you will quicken your new reality. If you react negatively you will hinder your progress. Once negativity seeps through into your mind, it plays tricks on you by telling you what you want will not happen, and it will give you all the reasons you want to back up its statement. Release negative statements, realise they are just a fear block and continue on.

3. Challenge old belief patterns — to eat or not to eat

BELIEF/THOUGHT: I feel so glad I gave up dieting, I feel free. I can eat what I want, when I want. Mmm, I'd love one of those chocolate biscuits.

ACTION: You eat the biscuit and then you say: "That was yummy! I feel satisfied with one. I know I can have another one whenever I want."

FEELINGS: Satisfaction, pleasure, contentment (knowing they will always be there).

BEHAVIOUR: You leave the rest of the biscuits. You put them back in the pantry. You go on to the next thing in your day without thinking about food.

See the difference! And it all started with a new thought to challenge your existing harmful thoughts.

4. Positive self-talk

Examples of negative self-talk: I must lose weight. I must lose ... kilos by ...

I have so much weight to lose, what's the point of even trying? I've failed all the time, what's the point of trying something new? I'm not losing weight, there must be something wrong with me. I'm putting on weight, I'm going to quit.

(a) Use a visual stop sign to change your negative self-talk into positive self-talk. If you are alone, shout it out — "STOP!" Clap your hands or do some gesture that to you means 'no more'.
(b) Take a few deep breaths.
(c) Close your eyes and bring the harmful words onto the TV screen of your mind. Now blow them away with gale force winds till they vanish from the screen in your mind. Once the wind dies down, bring up your positive self-talk and intensify it until it is dazzling with brilliance and is firmly etched in your mind.

Create a new positive self-talk dictionary

What are your new self-caring words going to be? Write them

down and learn them. Do your homework with change just as you did homework at school to learn. At least this is a subject you will enjoy studying!

My new dictionary:
I value and respect myself.
I care for myself.
I'm doing fine.
I accept slip-ups as learning experiences.
I love myself just as I am now.

Doing

Doing is the end result of thinking, writing and saying. If they have been effective, you will do or not do what you wish. If, for example, one of your affirmations was 'I now love and respect my body', and if you have been working mentally hard on this affirmation, you may find yourself having a massage or buying nice clothes. All the work you put in will give you such wonderful, empowering results. Persist — you owe it to your happiness and health.

Two books I recommend reading are *Absolute Happiness* by Michael Rowland, which will give you a great understanding of who you are and great techniques to bring about change, and *You Can Heal Your Life* by Louise Hay, which is a wonderful book on how to really love yourself, and gives some valuable insights into your behaviour patterns, plus exercises for growth.

HANDY HINTS

WORK CONSTANTLY, EVERY DAY, TO CHANGE YOUR BELIEFS.
TAKE ONE OR TWO OLD BELIEFS THAT HAVE THE BIGGEST INFLUENCE ON YOUR LIFE AND REPLACE THEM NOW.
REMIND YOURSELF: WHAT YOU ARE AWARE OF YOU CAN CONTROL; WHAT YOU ARE UNAWARE OF CONTROLS YOU.
START BECOMING AWARE OF HOW YOUR BELIEFS AFFECT YOUR EATING.

CHAPTER FIVE

BECOME MASTER
OF YOUR MIND

Dieter's belief: Losing weight — it's too hard to handle all the voices in my head.

'If only I could stop all the fighting inside my head, all I want is peace.' This is a thought we have with us most of the time when we are on the mad mouse wheel of dieting. We just want to stop all the arguing — it can drive us crazy. But I have some great news for you: you can make friends with these voices and when you do, watch the dramatic change in your life! You will be truly astounded at how quickly you can reprogram your inner voices to work for you, not against you. We are all made up of many different personalities and, wow, doesn't this make life interesting at times! One of the biggest voices that we deal with on the inside is our Inner Critic. We give it absolute power, especially when we have a weight problem. It is the one voice in us that has the ability to stunt our personal growth severely. Let's take a look at it in full swing.

You have gone out to lunch with friends and decide to forget the diet. You eat pasta with creamy sauces, finishing up with chocolate cake and full cream cappuccino. As you drive home in the car your Inner Critic starts up: "You're hopeless, how could you have eaten all that? Couldn't you have had just a little? No, you had to go the whole way. You are hopeless, you have no self-control, you will never lose weight. How many attempts is this? Just resign yourself that you are to remain fat. Oh, don't you feel sick — well, look who's to blame! And your friends will sure get a laugh out of it, too. You are indeed pathetic."

Sound familiar? It's very sad, really, as this voice is the one that stunts our growth the most. It is almost impossible to work on the issue of food and what it means to us when this voice has made our lunchtime get-together a major criminal offence. It makes us feel so bad about the cake and cream — humiliating and shaming us. You know this familiar pattern too well: our next issue is not food and how we use it to handle our stresses, it is now how to handle the attack of an out-of-control critical voice. And once this Inner Critic has reached the peak of authority, we find ourselves eating more to cover up the bad feelings that come from these critic attacks. Have a look back now at your dieting and weight-loss belief statements. How many of them are the voice of your Inner Critic?

Another voice we dieters hear a lot of, and which is best mates with our Inner Critic, is the Rule Maker.

Cafe scene, take 2, enter Rule Maker

"Do you know how much fat is in that dish you have just ordered? Now you will not be allowed to eat for the rest of the day. You probably consumed about 2000 calories and 100 grams of fat. Take a four-hour walk, drink water for the rest of the day, fruit tomorrow and we will take it from there!" This Rule Maker has become a Nazi nutritional expert; it has all the evidence at its fingertips and has great delight in telling you how intelligent it is. The problem is that it keeps food and your body at war.

The power of these voices is quite frightening. There is so much force and energy behind their words. Our first aim is to diffuse their power, and we do this by understanding who is speaking and that it is only one of your voices. Once you understand that you are not your Inner Critic and are able to separate from it and talk to it rationally, its power will greatly diminish.

Your Inner Critic's job is to help you live up to the standards set by your Rule Maker, who tends to sound like a mixture of your parents and society, but on the inside.

Now we add another inner voice which is part of this team: the voice of the Rebel.

Cafe scene, take 3

Your Rebel starts fighting against your Rule Maker, and the fight goes something like this:

Rule Maker: "Too much fat in that pasta dish, go for the salad."

Rebel: "Bugger off, you, I can eat what I like and I will. I will go for the creamy sauce, and I will top it off with chocolate cake and full cream cappuccino. That will shut you up for a while."

So there we have it: the work of the Inner Critic, Rule Maker and Rebel. Isn't it a pity they don't get along with each other? Life would certainly be a lot easier, wouldn't it? Struggles with food seem to be endless battles with these voices. This arguing inside our head will always bring a negative reaction. We will either give in to the Rebel, stuffing our face with chocolate and bearing the guilt of the Inner Critic later, or we'll give in to the Rule Maker, while underneath the Rebel will be seething, just waiting to get its turn.

We need to start making friends with these voices, and understand what is happening. I do not mean we have to psychoanalyse every craving for food, but just listen and try to do a bit of rationalising with these voices. As you gain experience at changing your old beliefs and start treating yourself kindly, you will begin to notice that you will be able to hear the voice of your Inner Wisdom, and the unhelpful subpersonalities will take a step back. Your Inner Wisdom is the one that has been buried for so long, drowned out by the other three. It is the one that speaks your gut reactions, the one that we have all been given at birth. Our Inner Wisdom is the voice that can argue the negative voices out of our head; see things as they are without delusion and emotion. The voice is instinctual, but like a baby who falls and then walks, we must give it the same tender loving care to bring it to its deserved place. Our goal is to bring this voice to the foreground again. Patience and awareness are the keys, and then a new thought pattern will arise in you.

Cafe scene, take 4

Rebel: "I want chocolate cake".

Critic: "No you don't".

Rebel: "Yes I do".

Rule Maker: "Do you realise how many calories and grams of fat there are in that huge slice?"

Inner Wisdom: "Okay, you lot, just knock it off for a few minutes, we are all going to try to get along to make my life a little easier. I need to think about this without you firing up. I think I really do feel like chocolate cake. I just need to put something in my mouth. I am feeling emotional."

Rebel: "Cut the psycho crap and give me chocolate!"

Inner Wisdom: "No, hold on, Rebel, why can't I handle thinking emotions?"

Me: "I feel angry when my friends are so thin".

Inner Wisdom: "Who is around?"

Rebel: "Yeah, look at Jennifer — that skinny bitch is always stuffing cream cakes in front of me. I want to do that, too."

Inner Wisdom: "So you become angry when skinny people are around and you want to eat to kill this feeling."

Me: "Do I still want to eat chocolate? Okay, I will have a piece and see how I feel. I just want some time out by myself."

See the difference it makes to an eating episode when the voice of your Inner Wisdom is in control? This is not always easy and not always possible. Do not try to analyse every eating episode; it can overwhelm you and you may want to give up. Remember, take small steps, start with the situations that seem to trigger the highest emotional state, those that set you off more quickly and more frenzied. I usually find women have a few predominant areas in which they need working on emotionally, and the eating binge coincides with this emotion. For example, anger = highly emotional, and goes with the biggest eating problem.

I strongly suggest working with a counsellor for a while to really change your behaviour patterns. Drs Hal and Sidra Stone have created a wonderful system called Voice Dialogue, which is aimed at understating and accessing different parts of yourself. It is a very powerful, simple method, best done with a Voice Dialogue facilitator. I recommend that anyone with a weight issue get to understand their inner selves. For me it was a great step forward in my progress.

HANDY HINTS

START LISTENING OBJECTIVELY TO YOUR INNER VOICES.

WRITE DOWN HOW MANY AND WHO THEY ARE.

START AN INNER DIALOGUE WITH THE MOST POWERFUL ONES.

CHAPTER SIX

ACCELERATE
YOUR PROGRESS

Learning anything new in our lives, no matter how simple, can be quite difficult because it not only involves physical actions but also mental awareness. How many times have you been on a diet only to revert back to old eating patterns? With the food halfway to your mouth, you think, "Oh, that's right, I am supposed to be on a diet". When we are on automatic pilot we are not aware of what we are doing. It requires a great deal of mental activity to be aware, so that we can change. Becoming aware is half the battle, the other half is persistence and taking a small step every day. Do not underestimate the power of your new beliefs and the techniques to implant them; they are simple, but very effective, and will bring about great change very quickly if practised regularly.

To assist your transformation
1. Keep a Journal
I can't stress enough the benefits of journal writing. There is so much chatting going on in your head, that sometimes it's hard to get a clear answer. Writing down your thoughts or feelings is a

positive benefit to your self-growth. Getting it out of your head and onto paper is a powerful process.

It doesn't have to be just words; you can draw or scribble thoughts when no words can describe how you feel. It's very theraputic to get it out of your mind. It will feel as if a real weight has been lifted.

2. Keep your attention fully in the present

Try doing the dishes without thinking of anything except the act of washing dishes. Just totally focus on what you are doing. See if you can last five seconds. It's just about impossible, isn't it? For most of us our minds run a million miles an hour thinking of what we need to do next, or worrying about what someone has said or done. How many times have you eaten something and, in a state of total shock, looked in the packet to find that all the biscuits are gone? "Where did they go?" you ask yourself as you swing your head from side to side to see if anyone is playing a trick on you.

Awareness, my dear friends, is the key. How can you change if you are not aware that you have to change? Most of us want to change as quickly as we can, only to find a week later we have tumbled back down further than when we started. The key is to get prepared for change — know what you are going to come across and know how to deal with it.

3. Be willing to explore your past to assist your future

Look into your family history and you will find a pattern. It is highly likely that someone in your family has a weight problem and has tried to lose weight. You will find that their belief systems are similar to yours — more than likely, they have indoctrinated you with them. One of my workshop participants told me that throughout her entire family history her mother, grandmother, great-grandmother and all the women in the family had always been overweight. She found it very difficult to conceive that she could ever lose weight. But the cycle must stop somewhere, the spell of this mind-set must be broken. You may find that you eat the same foods in the same way and in the same quantity that your mother did. My mother has a habit of spooning for herself the last bit of whipped potato and eating it at the sink before filling the pot with water. I always automatically do the same. But now that I am aware, I stop myself, usually just before the spoon hits my mouth.

4. Accept and like change
Activity: Resistance to change
With the hand you don't normally write with, write your name 10 times.

Did you think this was an exercise in futility? Did you give up because it was too hard? What other thoughts did you have? Whenever we are asked to try something new there is always fear — fear of failure. After all, we are all too familiar with diet failure, aren't we!

So the problem is, how we are going to get rid of this fear of failure so we have half a chance of success? You see, fear is always going to be there. When we leave our cozy safety zone we will always experience some fear and apprehension. Instead of being overwhelmed by it, however, we just need to alter its path so it becomes constructive, not destructive.

I am asking you to change your thinking; I am asking you to take five, ten, twenty or more years of harmful beliefs you have had about food and throw them out the window. That can be pretty scary because you have held onto them for so long; they have been your security blanket. To change your eating patterns requires you to first change your fundamental thoughts and beliefs about food, your weight and your eating. You know they do not help you, but you hold onto the comfort of familiarity, even when you know it is not very helpful. I know you could tell me how many calories are in numerous foods and the quickest way to lose five kilos, but has that ever helped you in the long run? I am asking you to implant a new set of eating and living values that will enhance the quality of your life and give you back your control and freedom.

5. Welcome setbacks and appreciate the lessons they give you

Look back over all your attempts at weight loss, and congratulate yourself for persevering for so long! My best effort was a loss of seven kilos in three weeks (however, I put on 10 kilos in the weeks that followed). I use to wonder how on earth I could eat normally and lose weight, when I couldn't even stick to a diet for a day. This hopeless reaction is a natural one when we try anything new to do with eating, so be prepared for it. We base our future expectations on past experiences. After all, what else do we have to compare them with? If your past experiences have all been failures, as in the case with dieting, then it's only natural to assume you will fail again. Success will look pretty difficult. That is why we move from diet to diet. However, there are a few things we must keep in mind:

- This is not a diet; this is a change in your thinking
- Do not ever compare your diet failures with this program
- You will always have setbacks

The word 'setback' does not mean failure. Do not class setbacks as failures — they are learning experiences. This is very important. Imagine telling children who fall off their bikes when they are learning to ride, "You can't ride if you fall off". Kids don't care, they will keep falling off until they get it right, however many times it takes to master. They get scratched and bruised, lose a bit of skin and pride, and off they go again.

Look how difficult learning to walk must be, but we all managed that with the greatest determination because we did not know what failure meant, and we had plenty of positive encouragement. As we grow up, people begin to tell us we can't do things and this starts seeding negatives in our minds. When we start to believe these negative thoughts, we go on a downward spiral. Be prepared — you *are* going to fall, but how you deal with the fall is very important. It is the key to your success. If you have a setback and then say, "I can't, this is too hard, I'm useless, this is just like a diet", you will send yourself down the spiral of despair.

6. Your progress will be up and down

Ups, downs and plateaus are normal progress phases for any changes you make in life. Most of us get very frustrated on the plateaus, thinking we are getting nowhere. Well, I will share with you a very important secret to success: Learn to love the plateaus as much as the ups. Plateaus are a sign of progress. No progress can be 'up' all the way, that's no challenge. Plateaus are there for a reason — to spur you on!

But learning experiences are never a waste of time. Imagine Greg Norman missing a putt. If this happened a few times in a row he could quite easily fall down the spiral of despair. Instead he reviews his setbacks constructively and learns from them to improve his game. The further you fall down the spiral, the harder it is to climb out. Just think back to a broken diet: the longer you binged, the worse you felt, and the harder it was to get back on track.

7. Always take mini-steps not giant leaps

When I gave up dieting I thought I could grapple all the new techniques at once. I'm impatient and I wanted instant results without the effort. The inevitable happened: I took on too much and my setback looked major. It is a bit like when you write a list of things to do in a day. You may have twenty items but because you only managed to accomplish six, you give yourself a hard time by concentrating on the fourteen things you did not do. We are so quick to give ourselves a hard time when we do not achieve all we set out to do, that we forget about all that we actually did do. We need to pat ourselves on the back for all the things we did do, no matter how small. To prevent huge setbacks we need to take small steps. Goals then become easier to reach and the likelihood of a setback is greatly reduced. If a setback does occur, it is only a stumble and it is a lot easier to get back on track. The importance of this step will be noticed later when we begin to change our eating patterns.

8. Willingly release the need to play victim

Who/what do you blame for your weight problem? Some answers that crop up continually in my workshops are:

"My husband. He keeps nagging me about my weight and he knows it just makes me eat more."

"If you lived in my household, you would be driven to eating, too."

"I worry too much about everything, eating helps me cope."

"If you worked around food all day, you would get fat, too."

"In my stressful job everyone eats sweets to cope."

"My boyfriend brings chocolates around, I can't throw them away."

Sound familiar? What we have here are a few typical 'Blame my weight on others/situations'.

Playing the victim role will never help you because what you are saying is "I'm not responsible for my weight gain; therefore, I'm not responsible for my weight loss either". We have to give up playing victim because victims always stay as victims; they never win.

It is understandable why we play victim. We feel so bad about being fat that blaming it on others or situations makes us feel better. However, these excuses just make things worse, because we believe these things to be out of our control and, therefore, we're helpless and cannot change them.

9. Continue to affirm love and acceptance of yourself

Change does not result from feeling guilty, angry, bitter, jealous or resentful. If you decide to lose weight with destructive thoughts as your driving power, weight loss is usually very temporary. One of my driving thoughts used to be jealousy. When I saw a slim figure I would rage with jealousy and start a diet only to finish with a stomach full of food and self-pity. You need to start trusting yourself, be willing to go on the journey, be willing to experience and learn from setbacks. You need to come from a place within you that is characterised by love, patience and understanding.

10. Forgive yourself when you go backwards

Isn't it weird how all of a sudden you can have a negative thought about your weight that seems to come from nowhere? You could be walking home and all of a sudden the thought hits you: "I am fat and revolting". You will then continue and justify the thought with, "Yes, yes, I am, and you know what else? I am …". Now with your new belief structure and your Inner Wisdom as your friend you need to change the direction of thought as soon as it arises. It may help you to bring into your consciousness your STOP sign every time a negative thought arises. This image will make you become conscious, and quickly. Remember, consciousness is the key to change. You must pick up on it instantly, however. It's no good before you go to sleep saying, "Oh yes, at lunchtime I had a negative thought — let's change it". This is too late. It has no impact. It must be in the present, at the moment, for it to do you any good.

Apologise to yourself for treating yourself so badly. Sometimes negative body thoughts are really abusive; they really have a nasty sting to them. Just write down a few when they arise and see for yourself. You would never give this sort of abuse to a friend, would you? You don't deserve such abusive treatment. In the past you may have used food as a painkiller but, as you start to become aware, you learn that kind words are much more effective.

Put the negative thought in a balloon and visualise it floating away and popping. Look closely at your thoughts and feelings and the scene that happened before or which will happen in the future. Your Inner Wisdom does want to take care of you and learn from mistakes. It understands your apprehensions and fears and wants to help. It is willing to examine every 'yes, but'. The old dieting devil will be there popping up all the time. Together you will figure it out. Remember, you are not alone. Your Inner Wisdom is loving, gentle, patient, kind and determined. Once you discover it, your wisdom will never let you down.

11. Place no harsh rules and conditions on your progress
Get rid of 'shoulds', 'coulds', 'musts', 'haves'. These only impose rules in your head and make your life a misery. Isn't it better to say, "I choose to lose weight", rather than, "I have to lose weight"? The 'have' is filled with desperation, frantic thoughts and fear. The 'choose' is filled with personal power, strength and determination. 'Willpower' is another word that conjures up thoughts of failure: "I'm hopeless, I can't lose weight. I have no willpower". Thoughts like these crop up because we are told time and time again that we have no willpower, otherwise we would not be so fat. But think of all the willpower you need just to stay on a diet for one day. People who do not diet say, "I don't see why it's so difficult — just stop eating so much". If only they knew. I don't like the word 'willpower' — it sounds like hard work. And if you fail, you're history — and hopeless. 'Control' also sounds too militant. Get rid of 'willpower' and 'control' from your vocabulary.

12. It is you and your persistence that are the keys to your success
You create the controls you need to succeed, and one of those controls is patience. Patience is a winner to success. Give yourself time — don't harvest the fruit before it is ripe and then complain it doesn't taste good. Give yourself time to fully accept new beliefs as being lifelong, not just a means to an end. Give yourself time to discover yourself. Gimmicks promise instant results with minimum effort. Nothing worthwhile happens quickly and without effort.

HANDY HINTS
STOP PLAYING VICTIM.
LET GO OF PAST FAILURES.
REALISE YOUR PROGRESS WILL BE UP AND DOWN.
TAKE MINI-STEPS NOT GIANT LEAPS.
PATIENCE AND KINDNESS ARE THE KEYS TO PERMANENT CHANGE.

PART TWO

A NEW
BEGINNING

CHAPTER SEVEN

CHECK OUT YOUR
EATING STYLE

Dieter's belief: I am not a 'normal' eater.

To get back to our natural eating patterns, let us first take a look at our current eating styles, as it is by recognising these that we get a greater understanding of our history of eating, and this understanding makes us better equipped for, and more accepting of change. Our eating style is greatly influenced by our childhood and family background.

To explore what influences have effected your eating patterns, answer the following questions: As a child, did you eat what you wanted? Were meal times enjoyable? Did you have to finish everything on your plate or else you didn't get dessert? Was food served in excess? Were some foods given to you to keep you quiet? Were some foods forbidden? Did you eat in secret? Were mealtimes tense? Were you a fussy eater? Were you ever asked what you would like for a meal? Were you ever cooked your favourite meals? Did you leave food on the plate?

How have these behaviours affected your current eating style?
Many of you will see patterns formed over the years which have moulded your behaviour with food. Which eating styles do you relate to?

Gobblers
If you are a gobbler you eat food very fast, wolf it all down, and get windy and over-full as a result. You eat quickly because you fear that you won't get your fair share, or that what you are eating is naughty, and you want to get it out of the way quickly before guilt sets in.

Sneakers
You eat accepted amounts and types of food in front of other people; alone you eat foods you consider as forbidden and/or large quantities of food. You are very concerned with what other people think, especially when it relates to food intake and body weight.

Bingers
You eat normal amounts at meal times and when you are around other people. However, a lot of your eating is out of control, fuelled by anxiety, and consists of forbidden foods when others are not around.

Clean-the-platers
I think we can all relate to this type of eating. Platers eat until nothing is left on the plate or table, regardless of appetite. This type of eating stems from most people's upbringing, where the sight of wasted food was a sin.

Nibblers, snackers
You eat normal meals but also many mini-meals throughout the day. You try to fool yourself that you don't eat much.

Stuffers
You stuff in as much as you can, maybe through fear, loneliness or diet deprivation. You are always trying to fill up that ever-growing void inside.

CHECK OUT YOUR EATING STYLE

Habitual eater
Your eating is habitual, by the clock and also by the type of food. You are the type of person who will eat a roast every Sunday, at 1 pm sharp. These are habits you have learned from your childhood and they stick deep.

Developing a normal eating style
To get back to your natural eating patterns you must first know what are considered natural/normal eating patterns. To help you do this, think of a time before you started dieting. You may have been very young, weight was not an issue, and neither were calories or nutrition. You ate what your body wanted, when it was hungry, and then you got along with the next thing in your day. You didn't think about food again until you were hungry. Can you remember those times? Think hard. Well, that is normal eating.

If you are still unsure, ask someone you know well who doesn't have an issue with food/weight the following questions: How do you know when to eat? How do you know what to eat? How do you know when to stop? Now they may look at you rather oddly, for eating to them is as natural as going to the toilet is for you. You do not spend all day thinking about when you should go to the toilet; your body tells you, and off you go, end of story. Remember, you ate normally at some stage in your life. Diets and emotional eating just got in the way somewhere along the line. You will return to this natural state. Your body is designed to take care of you, not destroy you. All it needs is for you to trust it.

HANDY HINTS
EXPLORE, AND LEARN FROM, YOUR EATING PATTERNS THROUGHOUT THE VARIOUS STAGES OF YOUR LIFE. OBSERVE A YOUNG CHILD EATING INTUITIVELY AND TRY EATING LIKE THAT FOR ONE DAY.

CHAPTER EIGHT

AWAKEN YOUR
SLEEPING POWER

Now that you know what natural/normal eating is, it is time for you to discover your own sleeping power within you. You are now going to learn how to get in touch with it again. It may feel a bit scary in the beginning because you will be living with no external rules and regulations. Trust your feelings; the wisest teacher and the only one for you is within. There is no greater intelligence than the one that is lying dormant in you at this very moment.

It is time now for you to be boss. Let your inner wisdom speak to you. It is frustrated that it has been denied its important role of looking after you. Give it back power. Diet authorities don't know your body like you do. You have the most intimate relationship with it, you know how it ticks, so isn't it obvious that you need to put yourself back in the driver's seat? The only way this will happen is if you start to break away from the external, detrimental rules you are using now to lose weight.

How long it takes before your natural eating cycle blossoms and you use its full potential depends on many factors, such as how long you have been dieting, how deeply entrenched is your dieter's mind-set, the company you keep, your level of self-esteem and trust, and your level of dependency on food as a way of coping with emotions.

Remember, your number one goal is to get in touch again with, and return to your natural eating patterns. Weight loss must become a secondary goal. Weight loss is bound to take place if you return to your natural eating patterns, so always keep that a top priority in your mind. The focus is on how you feel, not what you have eaten. If you continue to just focus on weight loss, you will get back onto the mad mouse wheel of diet-binge, and you will stop your progress.

Eating by your natural eating cycles is very different from dieting or restrictive eating. The main difference is that you are in total control of what you eat, when you eat and how much you eat. It's a great feeling of freedom.

HANDY HINTS

Borrow and read some books from the library on digestion (children's books are good) and learn about your body's digestive system. Draw the digestive system and label the parts. Observe the times of day you mostly get hungry.

CHAPTER NINE

STAGES ON YOUR NEW JOURNEY

During the discovery and mastery of your eating cycles, you will go through a series of stages, moving from one to another or being in a few at the same time. The important thing to remember is that this is a process, not a set of rules and regulations.

I cannot give you time frames, but provided you focus on nurturing yourself back to the power of your natural cycles, weight loss is inevitable. As you progress you will go through many different phases. I have listed them below to give you some kind of reassurance and comfort that you're not the only one feeling like this. You *will* start to gain an understanding of what you are going through, and why.

I started out with gusto and for the first few months things were going great. I thought, "yes, I'm there", and a day later I thought I was back to my old dieting days. I kept reminding myself that setbacks were inevitable, and not for the life of me was I going back to dieting. I picked myself back up and decided it was better to start with smaller steps, taking hold of one area and work on it before tackling others. My weight did fluctuate but the weight gains were nowhere near as drastic as they had been in my dieting days. Sometimes my weight seemed to stabilise for a while (which to me was a great achievement — not to put on weight when not dieting). After I got a grip on my new eating pattern, excess weight stayed off and my weight remained stable. Now my weight fluctuates slightly, depending on the season. You must remember how many years you have been in diet mode and that new beliefs and changes take time.

Phase 1 — Deciding to get off the wheel
Basically you are fed up and frustrated with dieting or restricted eating. You are frustrated with your unsuccessful attempts at weight loss, thinking that you are the problem, and are still on the merry-go-round of dieting. You have lost touch with your natural eating cycles and use food for every reason except physical hunger. You are not happy with your weight or your body shape and your self-esteem is at rock bottom. You begin to see the futility in the approach you have taken so far but don't know what to do. You are ready to get off the diet merry-go-round. You begin to understand why you have a weight problem and that diets will never help you permanently fix your issues. You know your issues are not directly related to food and your weight and that they go a lot deeper. You are ready to make a commitment to give up dieting, explore your issues, put food back in its proper place and re-learn to eat.

Phase 2 — Freedom!
You release yourself from diet jail with some apprehension. Once out you feel like a lion out of its cage, not knowing what to devour first. You eat foods that you normally totally forbid yourself to eat — as you make up for lost time. You find, in this phase, which could last a few days to a few months, that you begin to experience pleasures that food can give you again and, like a small child, you are in wonderment of all that is available to tantalise your taste buds. You then start to get in touch again with your inner wisdom and the roar of your hunger, only now you welcome it and work with it. A great sense of freedom and

self-empowerment comes over you. At times you feel a sense of desperation, lingering from the diet mind-set of not trusting that you can stop eating. You may experience a slight weight gain, but you must accept this as part of the process. If you don't, you will hinder your progress. Remember, this is a natural reaction from all your years of dieting.

Phase 3 — You begin to gain power
You begin to develop a greater trust in yourself and start to accept yourself and who you are. Feeling guilty about eating certain foods greatly diminishes, so does binge and secretive eating. Your weight starts to stabilise as you work with your Inner Wisdom. There is a great feeling about maintaining a stable weight. You are able to take just a bite or two of chocolate and feel comfortable leaving the rest, without any feelings of deprivation. You start to feel a personal power developing, with your newfound skill of controlling food.

Phase 4 — Weight loss happens and your life takes off!
Your start to lose weight. Yes, my dear friend, the one you have been waiting for: losing weight, eating what you want. Most of the time you eat when your hunger roars, feeling no guilt about the foods you choose. You are able to stop eating when you are satisfied, most of the time. Your self-esteem rises as you begin to explore and work out the personal issues that have held you back in the past. You want to learn more about self-growth and start venturing on a new path of self-development. You start to understand yourself a lot better and are able to trust and follow your feelings, which greatly diminishes your emotional eating.

You may find yourself in a few phases at the one time. There is no right way or time length. It is entirely up to you, the individual. However, the more you trust and are kind to yourself, the quicker your progress will be. What an exciting path to be on! So let's continue ...

HANDY HINTS

Get yourself mentally ready for your journey.
You might like to have a little ceremony
before you start.
Have something special or symbolic with you
that reminds you of your new journey.

PART THREE
KISS DIET DRAMAS
GOODBYE

CHAPTER TEN

SO LONG TO
SNEAK EATING

For you to get back on track and start eating normally again (the way nature intended), there are some important aspects to learn. In Parts One and Two, we have had a good look at the whole picture and realised that diets, restricted eating, the media, our culture and families, all mixed together with the belief systems we have formed, make a very potent cocktail for weight-loss failure. Working on changing your belief systems forms a major part of your success. In this section we are going to look at the harmful behaviours of sneaking, bingeing and feeling guilty about "forbidden" foods.

The damage caused by restricting our eating and playing the diet game — ignoring our natural instincts — leads to sneaking foods, bingeing on foods, and feeling guilty about eating certain foods. The more you turn away and bury your instincts, the more they will rebel. And what results are very painful sessions, battling with food, our emotions and weight. So let's explore the first culprit:

Dieter's belief: All 'forbidden' foods should be eaten in secrecy, away from the view of others.

The Sneaker: When the name of the game is not to get caught
We sneak foods for many reasons, the most common being that we are hiding from ourselves. We really don't want to know what and how much we are eating. Our sneaking then leads us to guilt and shame. When we eat secretly we are really only being harmful to the most important person, ourselves. All we are doing in reality is lying to ourselves. It seems quite absurd when we stand back and look at the lies we tell ourselves, the lengths we go to, the places we find ourselves eating. But that is what happens when we are not being true to our real feelings.

For many of us, eating is similar to stealing. We feel naughty and bad and we play games with ourselves to keep the truth hidden, because the truth is about fear and pain. So we distract ourselves with food.

Sometimes we sneak foods because we get a 'high' from sneaking and getting away with it. There is a thrill in not getting caught. When our lives lack spontaneity and fun, we start to create other ways — even detrimental ones — to fill that void. I remember the obsession with getting a 'score' of food when no one was around. Depending on my time frame, I would stuff in quickly what I could, and if I hadn't finished by the time someone arrived, I would spit out the remaining food inconspicuously. Being left on my own for a while was a chance to fit in as much as I could while no one was around. We time these sneaking/binge-type eating episodes with criminal calculation, knowing where to place the wrappers and how to get rid of all the evidence. Imagine how much guilt is inside us if we feel like criminals!

I want to share with you two types of my sneaking-food episodes that stick most vividly in my mind. The first type was the times I went to the toilet with a handful of chocolate eclairs, flushing the toilet whilst unwrapping the papers and eating them two at a time. I thought that was such a clever plan. However, I always got caught. My other type of episode was a ritual I used to follow when at work. I would buy a bag of soft toffees (because they were the ones I could eat the quickest and disguise the best) and hide them in my filing cabinet. Every time I wanted a fix, I just opened my filing cabinet, stuck my head in for a few seconds whilst I scoffed down a handful of toffees, and upon swallowing I would pull a piece of paper out of the cabinet. There I was, working and getting away with eating at the same time. I did this with the greatest of skill.

Can you relate to these two stories? In what places and situations have you found yourself sneaking foods?

Sneaking food seems a crazy, absurd and ridiculous thing to do, and it may be quite baffling as to why you do it, but start to think that there *is* a good reason. Ask yourself what you are trying to do or say by your sneaking. How does sneaking food help you? What does sneaking food protect you from?

For you to put an end to your sneaking food episodes you need to discover what it is you are trying to express with food. This has to be recognised before you can change it.

A story I tell in my workshops always brings a few laughs as others shyly admit to doing the same. The story goes: If on an eating episode I discovered or, more to the point, knew that there was a started block of chocolate in the fridge, I would start eating and, soon enough, the whole bar was just about gone. Feeling extremely guilty for eating so much and thinking how horrible it would be if anyone found out how much I really ate, I would proceed to finish off the chocolate bar. I would then go up to the local store, buy another one exactly the same, eat exactly as much as had already been eaten when I started, and put the rest back in the fridge, thinking that no one would ever know what had just taken place. The guilt and fear of being caught eating was tremendous.

If you don't allow yourself to eat in full view of other people, you are devaluing your self-worth and denying your needs. The common thought that goes with this action is 'if they see me eating fattening foods, they will then start thinking "no wonder she is fat; look at her eating that; how disgusting! She really shouldn't be eating that"'. We are so afraid of what people might think or say! Does it really matter what people think or say? You have to live with yourself 24 hours a day. Being true to yourself is the most important thing. We are all so afraid of someone telling us that we are fat because of what we eat. For it is very painful when this comes from someone else's lips; it goes right to the heart. But what is more painful — living a secret life of despair or coming out of the closet? Initially you will feel discomfort, but the freedom is terrific! You are not a criminal when you eat forbidden foods in full view of others — you are a hero!

Another reason we tend to sneak food is we don't allow ourselves time out to really enjoy eating certain foods. Because of our diet mentality and the guilt attached with eating such foods, our only hope lies in sneaking them, which then justifies our guilt. Can you imagine yourself taking 15 minutes to sit down with a cup of coffee and a piece of chocolate cake and enjoying it? How hard would that be? Most women think that to eat chocolate cake is bad enough, but to enjoy it, well that's outrageous! May I suggest that you do seriously try it? Normal eaters do it all the time, why can't you? It's part of your training. For the fact is, if you did this you would greatly diminish the times you sneak food and the quantities you eat. I see many women walking hurriedly along with one hand diving into their handbag and one in their mouth, trying to deny to themselves that they are eating at all.

We also tend to sneak food when we are too afraid to show our true self to others. Sneaking becomes a secret escape from the 'real world'. What then happens is that you start to alienate yourself from others and your secretive eating only escalates. You next start to convince yourself that something is really wrong with you and no one understands, so again you turn to food for comfort.

Sneaking food will continue until you have the courage to start being true to yourself and your feelings. A friend of mine told me a story of two very large ladies who worked with her. They always ate the 'right' foods at lunchtime and never ate morning or afternoon tea. No one could understand why they never lost weight, as they always said that they were on diets and doing well. Then one day my friend went down to the basement to get some papers and there on the floor were these two ladies, eating cakes — and so ashamed of being caught! That is very sad. So unlock the doors, banish sneaking and let food freedom into your life.

HANDY HINTS

Be true to, and honour, your inner feelings.
Be aware of what types of foods you sneak and why.
Try eating one food in full view, instead of sneaking.
Take the guilt away and learn from your sneaking episodes.

CHAPTER ELEVEN

BYE BYE
BINGE

Dieter's belief: If I start a binge-eating episode I may as well go the whole way.

Out-of-control eating, sneaking and eating forbidden foods go hand in hand to form one giant monster: 'the binge'! Bingeing is another back-lash caused by the dieter's mind-set and by playing the dieting game. To get rid of this backlash we must first understand what bingeing is and why we bring it into our life.

My binge-eating days I recall as a real nightmare. It was as if I had been taken over by a wide-eyed maniac who couldn't care less what was happening around me. Eating as much as I could was the only goal to reach. Afterwards I felt as if a cyclone had just been and gone. All the evidence was there on the outside in the form of empty paper wrappers and a very full stomach sticking out. But on the inside I did not really believe it had happened. The guilt that followed was absolutely HUGE — so big that some days I wouldn't even get out of bed.

What is bingeing?

To me, bingeing is out-of-control eating. It is a thought process which says that I have no control over myself. This type of eating is the feeling that my eating is so out of control that I will eat whatever I can lay my hands on, cooked or uncooked, frozen or not. A binge can be as small as four biscuits or as large as four packets of biscuits. Sometimes a binge can last one minute, sometimes one week. A binge session consists of eating so-called 'bad foods' and it is usually done in secret, hiding behind closed doors. Eating places can vary — from the toilet or the bathroom with the shower going, to the bedroom, under the sheets with the TV blaring. Bingeing and sneaking foods go hand in hand.

What makes the eating continue is the out-of-control thoughts that go with it. It's a feeling that 'I have been taken over by the devil and I can't stop'. There is a real urgency about wanting to eat. Binges happen quickly and are over before you know it, and all that is left to remind you that a binge took place is a mass of empty wrappers and crumbs and a person feeling very full and very depressed. It's like the morning after the night before: "Oh goodness, what happened? Did I really do that?" We are left with feelings of guilt, and the conviction that we are terrible, naughty and sinful.

What makes our eating go out of control?
1. Through the dieter's mind-set you deprive yourself of your physical needs, eating only certain foods that you believe to be good or guilt-free.
Again we see the backlash of not being true to our feelings, because depriving yourself physically of the foods you want or need increases your desire for them. Since most diets do not allow for our food choices, we immediately feel deprived. Often we binge because we are not allowed to have a certain food.

When we binge we feel we are naughty and bad for eating forbidden foods. When children are naughty and you tell them to stop, what do they usually do? They keep on going, rebelling against what they are told to do. Just as naughty children, we feel guilty and naughty for eating a bad food, and we keep on going. Sometimes we eat something, not because we want it, but because we have forbidden ourselves to have it. This then leads to guilt, self-hate and bad feelings. And when we feel low, what do we want? Comfort, of course. And how do we comfort ourselves? In the only way we know — eating.

When you give up dieting and restricting your food choices, this will greatly reduce feelings of physical deprivation. You won't go hunting for food when you give yourself permission to eat whatever it is you want. Once you stop dieting, the desire to 'have it all' greatly diminishes.

It is important to eat what you really want whenever you are hungry. This will greatly reduce the times you binge. After all, a trigger for a binge is eating something you feel you are not allowed to have. No more deprivation! You are not in a concentration camp! Really let yourself eat what you want, not what you think you should be eating. If it's ice-cream you want, a diet coke just will not do. When you really eat what you want, there is no need to 'eat it all now because tomorrow I won't be allowed to have it'. Binges are like last desperate attempts to get all of what you want before you can't have it any more.

2. Depriving yourself of your emotional needs

Not listening to your needs and feelings or experiencing an emotional low can lead to an emotional binge.

When you are in this state any situation can trigger a binge-eating episode. Many of you will be so used to depriving yourself in so many areas of your lives that convincing yourself that you need more self-care is quite difficult, especially in the area of eating. Most of us tend to believe we have overindulged and not deprived ourselves in this area. But until you convince yourself that you will never deprive yourself as you have done in the past, you will continue to overeat. Not only do you have to give yourself permission to eat whatever you want, but also give yourself permission to need whatever you need in other areas as well, regardless of whether or not your needs are met. There is no such thing as needing too much, whether it is food, love, compassion or comfort. Having time out is not selfish nor has it anything to do with how good, bad, fat or thin you are or what you did or didn't do that day. We all deserve time out, but before you take time out you must first acknowledge that you are worthy of having that time.

Sometimes our emotional hungers are so deep we just keep on eating, never feeling satisfied. Bingeing is a sign that we need more, not less, time out for ourselves.

List how you keep yourself emotionally deprived. For example: I don't ask for time out when I need to be alone. I say 'yes' when I want to say 'no'.

When you binge for emotional reasons you need to reassess how you are taking care of yourself. Maybe you need some time to yourself. Women, generally, have many responsibilities and having some time out is necessary to recharge your batteries. My remedies for recharging my batteries are taking an aromatherapy bath with my favourite music on, giving myself a facial, going window shopping and buying something like a crossword magazine, watering the garden and playing hose with my dog, walking round the neighbourhood and looking at gardens. There is nothing worse than taking time out only to be feeling guilty and thinking of what you should be doing!

Make a list of ways you like to recharge your batteries. They can be fun, silly or meaningless, so long as they are things you love doing. Take one activity from your list and do it once a day.

1st Aid for a Binge
This is for when you find yourself knee-deep in food, frantically eating, wanting to stop so badly but wanting to continue eating just as badly.

1. Become aware of yourself
Picture this scene: You have had a difficult time with someone at work who drives you crazy, yet you haven't said anything. Seething with anger, you arrive home. No one is around. You sit down exhausted for a few minutes and turn on the TV. You get up and check out the kitchen cupboards. There are lots of different foods that you don't permit yourself to eat. You decide to settle on some cracker biscuits, but that doesn't seem to satisfy

you. You move to sweet biscuits, chocolates and before you know it, you are eating frozen cheesecake. Picture this vividly in your mind.

Now I say to you, "Stop moving and sit down". Reluctantly you obey my demand and you suddenly realise that you are, in fact, having an uncontrollable eating episode. You think to yourself, "Oh gosh, what am I doing?" Immediately you try to hide from the fact that you are doing this. Don't try to hide from the fact that you are eating.

You feel as if you have been shaken out of a drunken stupour, dreamland. You wake up and realise that you are not dreaming and you are eating. You now accept the fact of what you are doing. You can stop or keep going — the choice is yours. Until you become aware of bingeing, you won't have a chance to do anything else.

2. I now tell you to give yourself the OK, to keep eating

You look at me strangely. Your immediate impulse is to deny that any activity took place. You don't want to go back to square one. You want to deny all your eating because you feel it's not okay to binge and you really are bad, naughty and deserve to be punished. As you have these thoughts you start to eat again, and you begin to realise if you keep up this thought pattern, you will keep eating to console yourself. You finally allow yourself to binge. The strangest thing starts to happen: you can actually taste the food. The decision to continue or not is up to you.

3. Start to become aware of food

You begin to notice taste, smell, texture and what it feels like to eat. Are you enjoying the food? Get in touch with your body again. Try to come back to the present. As you are alone, I ask you to talk to the food. Tell it how you are feeling and what you are wanting it to make you feel or not feel. You tell the food you want it to make the anger and frustration go away. You begin to feel terribly sad, realising it cannot do this.

4. Become aware of your body
Stop for a few seconds and touch your body — arms, legs, face. Take a few deep breaths and try to come back to the present. Go and look in the mirror. What do you see? Touch your face, breathe deeply, smile and remind yourself that you are in the present.

You decide to stop eating and you are feeling extremely fragile, and your feelings of guilt, low self-esteem and self-hate are at their highest because you are equating eating with your self-image. You immediately have thoughts of starving yourself. Before you have time to think more, I say to you to be extra kind and special to yourself now! Treat yourself with kindness more than you have done in the past. This is the time when you really need to be with yourself; this is the time your Inner Critic and Rule Maker will be at their strongest. Don't give in to their abuse. Counteract their scolding with your new mind-set and positive thoughts.

Do something extra special for yourself; treat yourself — without the guilt. We usually tend to do the opposite after a binge and be twice as hard on ourselves. That just quickens the pace to another binge and tightens the noose further. Decide to take a walk in the park and do some deep breathing.

5. Now, forgive yourself
You binged because you didn't know what else to do. Do not deprive yourself of food when next you eat — that is just punishing yourself. What now happens is our Inner Critic comes to the fore with seething abusive remarks and the Rule Maker comes in also to tell us we are never allowed to binge again! We then listen and obey our Rule Maker and create severe, restrictive diets to balance out the binge. I cannot ever remember a time when I actually followed through with an after-binge diet. It was just too severe and it only led to another binge, tightening that noose of self-hate even further.

The best thing you can do is to eat again when you are hungry. You need to develop that trust in yourself again by reminding yourself that you can take care of your body, and that eating what you want does not make you fat.

6. Learn from each uncontrolled eating episode

Remembering a binge can help you realise what triggers you into a feeding frenzy and why. As painful as reliving a binge is, it is also the key to stopping. You need to understand why the binge happened in the first place. Try to remember your last binge.

What made you binge? What were you doing? How did eating feel for you? Where were you? Who was around? What did you eat? Where did you eat? How fast did you eat? What made you stop eating? How did you feel after the binge? Write down the insights that came out of this exercise. These insights are important. A binge is never a waste of time if you can learn from it. A binge is to really be looked into closely, as under the act of eating there will always be a real need to take care of yourself. The eating is just the surface stuff. Look deeper and you will find there is an urgent need to take care of yourself in some way.

Beliefs on bingeing

Write down your beliefs on bingeing and the preceding thought and action. You will begin to see just how harmful your beliefs really are to your well-being. Write out a new set of beliefs to counteract the old, harmful ones.

Belief
Bingeing is a lack of willpower and discipline.
Time out for yourself is selfish.
To stop bingeing you must punish yourself and work harder.

Action/Thought
Start feeling really bad and guilty.
Busy myself even more so people don't think of me as fat and lazy.
Start going frantic, eating less, not buying clothes and denying all treats.

A word about trigger foods

Many of us blame certain foods — mainly chocolate — for triggering a binge, claiming we are allergic or that it is addictive. In my experience, the more you eat, the more you want, the more you crave. At certain times of the month you may crave more, but that is not permission for an all-out binge — that's a cop-out. I have had food allergy tests myself and have found when I have eaten massive doses of chocolate, I am more prone to an allergic reaction. The key is moderation, and permission to eat whatever it is you want.

The most common causes of bingeing are psychological, with only a slight element of physical — such as a low blood sugar level. Observe when it is you crave certain foods, such as at certain times of the month or certain times of the day or in certain situations. Be aware and you will find a pattern. I now find that one small lolly or one small bite of something sweet is enough to satisfy my sugar craving. Become aware that you don't have to eat the whole cake or chocolate bar to satisfy a sugar craving. Do it once and you will start to realise how easy it is when you put a few things into practice.

HANDY HINTS

REMEMBER AND LEARN FROM YOUR BINGE — AS PAINFUL AS IT IS, YOUR INSIGHTS WILL HELP YOU IN THE FUTURE.

DO SOMETHING DAILY FROM YOUR 'TIME-OUT LIST'.

TREAT YOURSELF WITH SPECIAL KINDNESS AFTER A BINGE.

EAT THE FOODS YOU REALLY WANT TO EAT.

CHAPTER TWELVE

TAKING THE 'GUILT'
OUT OF FOOD

Dieter's belief: I cannot control myself around forbidden foods — they control me.

The third damage from the dieting mind-set is the 'guilt food game'. The advertising and diet industries have categorised foods into two categories for us: 'good' and 'bad'. The 'good' foods are high in fibre, low in fat and low in kilojoules. Whereas the 'bad', 'sinful', 'wicked' and 'forbidden' foods are laden with fat and calories — chocolate and ice-cream fall beautifully into this category, and they are always advertised as sinful and wicked: 'be a devil and indulge'. However, we are told that we are not allowed to eat them because we are fat, and the diet rules are that we must only eat the good foods, such as salads and fruit and low-fat crackers, just as all the other good, thin people do. No wonder we feel so naughty if we indulge in these so-called bad foods. Why, if they are so bad and we shouldn't eat them, do they outnumber the so-called good foods ten to one? Everywhere you look there are chocolates, ice-cream, chips, biscuits. Whole aisles in supermarkets are dedicated to one type of item. Shops are dedicated to ice-creams and chocolates. And no one eats these? Come on, who are they trying to kid?

Our dieter's belief about these so-called bad foods is 'all or nothing': "I have eaten three, I may as well do a proper job and finish the lot off. And what's more, I put on weight just looking at them". We have become paranoid about these foods, thanks to the help of the media and diet industry. However, the more you forbid yourself certain foods, the greater the likelihood that you will binge on them. Your rebel voice is seething, saying, "Listen here, don't keep denying me what I want to eat or what you think I want to eat, because when I get my hands on it, I ain't gonna let you stop."

With this type of 'forbidden food' mentality we begin to think that some foods have a magical power over us. They literally talk to us through glass windows, fridges and shop shelves, all saying the same thing: "eat me". This type of thinking may have been with you for many years, even down the generation line to your mother's thinking. I have found that this is quite a difficult dieter's belief for a lot of women to break away from.

It is time to implement a new belief right now.

New belief: No food has power, no food is magical. I am in control of food; it no longer controls me.

We binge on forbidden foods because we do not allow ourselves to eat foods freely. You are not going to gain 20 kilos by letting yourself eat chocolate some of the time. In fact the opposite is true: by allowing yourself to eat your forbidden foods whenever you want, they lose their magical power. They become ordinary. You know that you can have them whenever you want, and the need to binge disappears. Remember, one of the main reasons for bingeing is depriving yourself of the foods you really want.

Exercises
My guilt foods
To get rid of your harmful dieter's beliefs you must first do some exercises to make foods 'ordinary' again. Firstly, make a list of your forbidden/guilt foods, foods you do not allow yourself to eat freely or without guilt. Look at your list and decide which foods

you would like to eat again without feeling guilty. Do you think you could dare to bring one of those foods into your house? Try it. And what's more, buy a lot of the food you have chosen, more than you could eat in one go. The reason for doing this is very important. Our diet mentality does not allow for us to have a huge amount of food around. We are shocked at the idea and scared that if we see a small portion we will polish the lot off because we have no willpower. We are breaking that mind-set now with the idea of abundance, so we will be inclined to panic less, for the food will always be there and we can eat it when we please. It is not an all-or-nothing drama anymore.

The aim here is to eat that food when you feel like eating it, then stop when you have had enough. Make sure you allow yourself the pleasure of good taste. If you love chocolate, buy the best that you can afford. (My favourite is Lindt — mouth-watering stuff.) As you begin to eat your forbidden foods, notice whether you like them as much as you thought you would. Notice how they taste now that you know they are going to be freely accessible and that they have lost the 'forbidden' tag . Remind yourself that you can have these foods again, anytime you wish, when you are hungry. Gradually go through your forbidden foods list and reintroduce a new food into your kitchen weekly. If this is too difficult, do it at your pace. Maybe once a month is enough for you.

You may be thinking that I've gone quite mad: "First, Di, you tell us not to diet again and now you're telling us to bring ten bars of chocolate into our house? Are you nuts?" You only think this because of your deeply ingrained 'dieter's lack of trust' in your mind-set. That is understandable after so many years of dieting.

You will initially have a strong resistance to eating guilt foods: "Won't we want to eat all this food because we know it's there, and it will always be staring us in the face when we open the fridge or cupboard?" you might ask. The answer to this question is: "yes and no". Initially you may be tempted to eat that particular food when you see it. But remember that you are breaking a very harmful, deeply embedded dieter's belief. After a short time the novelty does wear off. Food does start to lose its magic and you will eat less of this food because it has become ordinary and plentiful. If you kid yourself and think, "I'm not going to do this exercise — my forbidden foods are always in the shop, out of sight, out of mind", you are not being true to yourself, and these foods will always have a magical hold over you.

So off you go to the supermarket and buy five, two-litre tubs of ice-cream. As you put them in your freezer you start to panic. You feel that this is crazy — you want to *lose* weight, not put it on. You sit down in a state of panic and start to eat the ice-cream in a frenzy. You do this two or three times and then you begin to realise and understand why you must do this exercise. You realise that it is absurd that you let these foods have control over you. If you really do want to stop bingeing and get control, you really do have to conquer your obsession. After a few weeks you start to feel that you are getting control. You continue to eat your favourite food and persist with the uncomfortable feelings. You begin to concentrate more on taste, texture, the feeling of fullness. You know the food is always there and you are not eating out of fear and feeling out of control.

After a while the novelty wears off: "So what if this is a big scoop of chocolate ice-cream! Big deal if this is a dry biscuit. Food is just food; I'll eat what I want. It might be a piece of chocolate or it might be an apple." You are now at the stage of trusting yourself. It is a wonderful feeling as the freedom starts to develop in yourself. You now control the food; it no longer controls you. It is not all that you made it out to be.

Hints to help

1. Put foods in their appropriate place

Any food you want to eat should be kept at home with plenty of it available. Make sure these foods are kept in their appropriate space such, as the fridge, pantry, etc. The whole aim here is to keep these now legalised foods in the appropriate place so that the decision process to eat or not to eat takes place when you are ready to eat, and so that the foods not in their appropriate place do not trigger off other eating. When– and only when– you allow forbidden foods in your house in abundant quantities will you truly master them.

2. Learn to enjoy the childlike art of eating 'forbidden foods'
I remember when I brought into my house ten packets of Chocolate Royal biscuits. As a child I used to smash the biscuit on my head, peel off the chocolate, suck out the marshmallow and nibble the biscuit. As an adult I used to binge on them, eating the whole biscuit, never enjoying them. Chocolate Royals were one of my forbidden foods. I decided to reclaim my childhood habit of eating Chocolate Royals so I ate them for breakfast, lunch and dinner for three days straight. I then started to crave fruit and salad — first time for everything! I still eat Chocolate Royals the way I used to as a child and I find that one biscuit more than satisfies me — and I have fun eating them.

If you are on a special eating program due to medical reasons, work as broadly and creatively as you can within your constraints. Remember the key point on change — trust yourself. If hot chips and pizza is on your list and it's impractical to bring those foods into your house, find out where the nearest shop is (you probably know them all anyway) and allow yourself permission to go there whenever you want to.

3. Crack your dieter's mind-set — beliefs that have to go
(a) 'Guilt food means junk.'

It is quite common for people when they get to this stage to fill up their cupboards only with forbidden foods. It is important that you go beyond the foods that you have always forbidden yourself to eat and really try to figure out what it is you want. You have to break down all food barriers and even legalise non-fattening foods so that you can eat them without feeling punished or deprived. That means one day you will squeal with delight at how wonderful a baby tomato tastes when it pops in your mouth and you will enjoy the creamy, rich taste of a chocolate mouse with only one thing on your mind: pure enjoyment and delight. Try finding foods you truly find appetising, regardless of calories or fat intake.

Karen, a women at one of my workshops, suddenly found out that she really enjoyed Mediterranean food and, like a child with a new toy, had great delight discovering the wonderful tastes and textures of these foods.

(b) 'Guilt foods mean guilt feelings.'

For our old habit of emotional eating to serve its purpose, we need to have guilt foods. Let me explain further: Say your friend rings you and tells you a new man is taking her on an overseas trip for three months. Part of you is thrilled for her but, at the same time, you experience conflicting emotions, such as envy and jealousy. These feelings of competition make you feel very uncomfortable. So rather than allowing yourself to feel these feelings that you consider bad, you reach for bad foods like the chocolate mint slices in the fridge. When you finish eating the packet of mint slices, you scold yourself and tell yourself how bad you are for eating such bad foods. It's easier for you to feel bad because you have eaten a bad food, than it is to feel bad because you are envious of a good friend. When you make all food legal and take away the 'good' and 'bad' labels, you diminish their power. Then you can no longer use 'bad' foods to hide what you really think is bad about yourself. If you have feelings that you feel guilty owning, it is difficult to keep food guilt-free.

(c) 'My health is at risk.'

Many women think it utterly against all the rules to eat their forbidden foods: "It's so non-nutritious, so unhealthy, so unbalanced." I am sure, however, that you can think of many binge days that were worse than your most unhealthy nightmare. The important thing to remember is that it is far better to go through a few weeks of eating food that is less nutritious than to spend a lifetime emotionally and physically depriving yourself by dieting. No one has a 'perfect' diet.

Are you denying yourself certain foods out of fear or as a result of some health-based belief? If you feel you are addicted to sugar and sweets, you will want to remove them completely from your diet. But this will just make you have an exaggerated yearning for sweets. And once they're removed from your diet, you will binge because you have made them forbidden, not because you are addicted. My friend Sarah is always on and off sugar. There is no in-between; it's full-out eating or total deprivation. Her mind-set needs to be changed, as she is going nowhere fast. Whenever you eliminate foods because of fear, you will feel like a junkie in withdrawal. You will binge on those foods at any opportunity. In my experience, when people really allow themselves to legalise all food, they end up choosing a wide variety of healthy foods that makes them physically and mentally alive. Of course if you have a medical condition, you will need to modify your diet.

Also, remember that the thoughts you associate with certain foods impact on your mind as well as your body. If you believe 'this food is bad', this belief will make you feel bad in both your mind and body. I grappled for many years with my guilt feelings about chocolate. It was all or nothing. I could never find a happy medium. Some 'experts' told me to give it up completely, some said to substitute it with carob, others advised to just allow myself small quantities. In the long run I figured it out myself — again by listening to my Inner Wisdom, who said it felt okay to eat small quantities, but that if I fed my body too much, it would get slow and sluggish. I have since found my ideal relationship with chocolate. What's more, I only buy the best quality, which has fewer additives than some cheaper brands.

(d) 'I cannot indulge in the idea of having all these foods around me.'

We all feel good around things we like. We surround ourselves in our home with nice furnishings and special knickknacks that make us feel good. So why don't we do the same with food? The sooner you can create a pleasing environment with food, the sooner you will relax around it. Many women feel that buying more food than they could possibly eat is a terrible waste. Remember, you are buying your favourite foods for eating and enjoying, and the surplus is there to remind you that you are taking care of yourself, giving yourself support and permission to eat. Think of your surplus food the way you would your favourite flowers. You feel happy and comforted just looking at your flowers. Your favourite foods serve their purpose both by just being there and by being eaten. The more you allow your foods to be legal, the more you allow yourself to bring them into your home, the less frantic you will feel about eating it all.

You may find yourself getting annoyed at having all this nice food around, and you might find yourself slipping back into old patterns, such as wanting low calorie yogurt instead of ice-cream. You then start wanting less food around you, and slowly the panic starts again. All these feelings signal your reluctance to completely let go of your old dieter's mind-set. If it feels good to surround yourself with nice things, why not surround yourself with nice food? If you allow your supply of all the foods you love to eat get low, you are giving the power back to these foods and once again they become forbidden. When food simply tastes good and is available, rather than being special but forbidden, it is no longer an effective painkiller. So you can see that you do suffer a certain loss as you conquer your eating obsession. The minute it begins to feel that food is powerful, it is time to re-stock.

(e) 'My family will ridicule me.'

Another problem you may face is with the people in your house. Many of you will be scared of their reactions or ridicule. Comments like, "Great diet this one: eat all you want. I've heard everything, but this really takes the cake — no pun intended." Or, "Great diet. This is really about family participation. I'll help you eat all this food."

There are a few ways to tackle these situations: You can keep your goodies in a brown paper bag with your name and 'hands off' or 'Poison' written on it. You can buy extra food, so no one will complain.

Tell other family or household members about what you are doing.

I decided to play it down and I told my family: "Never mention the word 'diet' again and neither will I. From this day on I am never going on another diet. I am just going to get on with my life." Quite often we draw attention to our plight because we keep harping and wingeing about losing weight.

You may like to get your partner to read this book so he or she will have a better understanding of what you are doing. It is up to you.

So enough of the guilt-food police — it's time to break out and bring back the word 'delicious' to describe all types of food. Liberate yourself. Just dare to for one day and you will be amazed at the change in your life and the freedom you feel.

HANDY HINTS

ALLOW YOURSELF TO EAT ALL FOODS FREELY.
GET RID OF THE WORDS 'FORBIDDEN FOODS' AND 'BAD FOODS' FROM YOUR VOCABULARY.
TRUST YOURSELF — YOU WILL FEEL UNEASY AT FIRST, BUT THE NOVELTY WILL WEAR OFF.

PART FOUR
YOUR STEPS
TO SUCCESS

CHAPTER THIRTEEN

YOUR BODY
KNOWS BEST

Your steps to success (what they don't teach you in diet school)
Up to this point you have been given valuable information to bring about the changes in your thinking and techniques to help you overcome and change the harmful dieter's mind-set. Awaiting you now are the steps you will need to master the outer world, the world of food and eating. Once you become the master of these steps, life will do a turnaround for you. It is such a wonderful, liberating experience — being able to eat what you desire, when you desire it and how much you desire. Knowing that you are the one in control gives you a feeling of self-empowerment and satisfaction that is incredible.

One question that has probably been in your mind from the beginning is 'How will I know what to eat if no one tells me?' The answer is simple: trust your body; it knows what is best for you. We all want a long, healthy life, full of vitality. If I knew the perfect foods for fulfilling this wish, I would say, "Let's go for it!" The reality is that every health expert says they know the magic foods for a healthy life. They believe these foods are right for them, but they may not necessarily be right for you. We are more confused than enlightened. What I know for sure is that your state of mind is just as important for a healthy life as the food you put into your body. I also know that if you deny certain foods for health reasons, you crave them — and this leads to bingeing. When I legalise all foods, I crave them less and can figure out what my body needs from the inside out.

SO LET'S BEGIN BY INTRODUCING YOU TO YOUR SUCCESS STEPS:

1. Eat when you are physically hungry.
2. Eat foods you really feel like.
3. Provide yourself with a great selection of foods.
4. Sit and eat slowly in a calming atmosphere.
5. Stop eating when you are satisfied.

In the following chapters, each step will be explained in detail and you will be given techniques to help you gain success with these steps.

Before we start with step one, there is just a little more preparation to be done. We must get rid of two diet tools and the belief that accompanies them, for they greatly hinder our process.

Tool one: the calorie counter (internal and external)
Dieter's belief: Dieting and counting calories is the only way to lose weight.

By now I think I have said enough to convince you to stop dieting and that also includes counting calories. Counting calories is a futile exercise; it takes all the fun and pleasure out of eating, making it seem like a chore and a miserable activity. When I was in my diet mentality, I would sit down to something I really enjoyed eating, look at the packet to see what it contained in energy value (kilojoules), and immediately the guilt would set in. I would cease to enjoy the food instantly. Again, the power of the diet mentality turned an enjoyable eating episode into one full of guilt and self-hate.

After so many years of being told what to eat, to suddenly stop dieting and counting calories are hard habits to break. One lady in my workshop was incredible when it came to calorie counting: she could put a calorie and fat value on every food I mentioned. Most of us, to some degree, know the ins and outs of certain foods and their calories. If knowing about and eating by calorie content is supposed to make us thin, surely all of us would be! People without a weight problem (in mind and body) would not have the foggiest idea about calories and couldn't really care less. That goes for fat counting too!

Tool two: the bathroom scales
Dieter's beliefs: I must weigh myself at least once a day.
Scales will dictate my mood for the day.

How crazy are we to give such control to a small piece of man-made machinery! It really is comical when you think of how much power we give to the humble bathroom scales. We talk to them, we beg and plead with them, we hide them, we move them around different floor surfaces — all so that they will magically tell us we weigh less than we thought we did. Scales often give you an inaccurate reading of your weight through the fault of the scales or through the cheating we do, such as turning the dial back past zero or moving the scales around different floor surfaces to get the best reading. That half a kilo creates a 'do or die' situation, and we tell our friends, "Oh my god, I've put on half a kilo!" "Half a kilo," they say, "oh yes, I can see that". Really, how absurd is that! No one in a pink fit could see if you had put on half a kilo, and who really cares anyway? I used to have one hand on the bathroom bench to get a lower reading or just fantasise that I only weighed 55 kilograms. I know a woman who used to weigh herself ten times a day. She even took mini scales away with her on holidays! Her scales totally dictated her moods for the day. When we allow scales to turn a great day into a miserable one, or a miserable day into a great one, it's time to reassess our lives and get rid of the scales!

Now seriously, what is the real benefit of knowing what you weigh? Who really cares? Let's face it, I don't know any woman who has a great relationship with her scales. It seems to be one of love, hate and deceit. Your Inner Wisdom couldn't care two hoots what you weigh. Knowing your weight only makes your ego paranoid. It serves no purpose except to keep the scale manufacturers in business. You must learn to start accepting your body, regardless of how much it weighs.

How much you weigh is irrelevant. Look at Elle McPherson. Do you wonder how much she weighs? Does it matter? If we see a slim woman whom we envy, we rarely ask ourselves, "I wonder how much she weighs?" We usually say, "I wish I were as thin as her". I haven't weighed myself for 15 years. Occasionally I have had to be weighed for medical reasons, but I couldn't care less what I weigh. I'm happy inside and out — that's what is important. Get rid of this destructible habit of scale watching. It serves no purpose whatsoever and only adds fuel to your diet mentality paranoia. Don't go from scale-watching to body-measuring — that is just as bad. If you really want to know if you have lost weight, try on some clothes.

If you find it very difficult to throw your scales away, at least try putting them out of sight or stick a piece of paper over the reading that says 'You are beautiful and you are your ideal weight' or 'I love you just as you are, I don't need to know how much you weigh'. Make sure you stick it down well so you are not tempted during weak moments. The only thing you should ever weigh is your suitcase at the airport when you go on that holiday you earned from the money you saved by not buying scales, rowing machines, diet drinks, diet memberships and pills. Now we are ready to embark on the journey to discover the great experience of intuitive eating. Let's begin!

HANDY HINTS
GET RID OF SCALES IN THE BATHROOM.
PICTURE IN YOUR MIND YOUR IDEAL SIZE.
ENJOY FOOD WITHOUT READING LABELS.

CHAPTER FOURTEEN

YOUR HUNGER
IS YOUR BEST FRIEND

Success step 1: Eat when you are physically hungry.
Dieter's belief: Suppress hunger at all costs.

How many times have you heard people say, "I am so hungry I could eat a horse" or "I am so starved I have gone beyond the point of hunger"? Your physical hunger is not something to suppress. This is one of the great errors that we have learnt from the weight-loss industry. Dieting teaches us to ignore our hunger calls and drown them out with hunger suppressant tablets, drinks, bulking agents, gum, cigarettes. What we are doing is fighting the very thing that can save us. I know many women who get a high from feeling hungry all the time. "It shows discipline", they say. To me it shows stupidity.

Years of dieting and being told when, what and how much to eat gradually take their toll, and the price you pay is eating for every other reason except the crucial one: physical hunger. You have forgotten that eating has something to do with being hungry. Most of the time you eat in response to your mind and thoughts, paying little or no attention to your body's needs for physical nourishment. Eating when you listen to your hunger growls is crucial because on the deepest levels it registers that you are beginning to trust and follow your natural bodily instincts;

that you are starting to take care of yourself on the most basic, fundamental level.

What is hunger?
Hunger is heat: your digestive fires burning hot and telling you they are ready for food. Get to know your hunger well, befriend your long-lost companion. It is lonely and rusty and needs to be worked rigorously to utilise its maximum potential. Feeding yourself when you are hungry is the most primal of all instincts. It is living in harmony with your body's cycles, in sync with nature. Hunger is your friend, not your enemy. When you fight your appetite, you are fighting the laws of nature.

From early morning till noon your body is in the phase of ridding itself of waste and food debris. This is why we generally have a bowel movement in the morning. Your metabolism in the morning is fairly low, but by lunchtime, noon, when the sun is high in the sky, your metabolism is at its peak. This is when your body can burn up food the quickest, so it is wise to do most of your eating from noon till 6.00 pm.

After 6.00 pm your body slows down, in sync with the setting of the sun, and begins absorbing and using the foods. When you eat by your natural body cycles you will find that you will be hungry when your metabolism is at its highest. As digestion of food takes up more energy than any other body function, it is wise not to eat too late. As a general rule, make your cut-off no later than 8.00 pm, for after that time your body is doing little activity, metabolism is low and your body cannot make the best use of the food you have given it, so it will store the excess as fat. I know that if I eat after 8.00 pm, my tummy will always feel squirmy and bloated. If I eat before 7.30 pm, I am fine. I like light meals in the evening as a general rule. Our bodies work in cycle with nature — this is a key point to remember.

When you feed your body, listen to the signals it gives you. It will tell you whether it liked what you fed it or not. Trust and observe. You know your body best. I may like milk and suffer no mucous, you may drink milk and be phlegmy all day. You may like sardines, I don't — they repeat on me for hours. Our tastes are very personal.

The very basics of digestion

Did you know your stomach is the size of your fist? It is like a collapsible bag, which lies in folds when it is not full. Digestion starts when you say, "Mmm, that smells good." This happens because your stomach is under hormonal control, and the mere anticipation of food starts digestion juices flowing. The smell of food stimulates the release of saliva in your mouth and gastric juices in your stomach.

Don't rush eating, because food needs to be chewed thoroughly — it needs to be masticated, making digestion and nutrient absorption more efficient.

After you have eaten and your stomach is full of food, it will protrude. The more you have eaten, the more it will protrude, as we all know too well. It takes about four hours for your stomach to empty after a meal. Carbohydrates are liquefied and then passed into the upper section of the small intestine where nutrient absorption occurs. When the remains pass into the lower intestine, all nutrients have gone and your wastes are ready to be excreted. When you go to the toilet and you see bits and pieces of food in your faeces, that means you haven't chewed enough and the food has slid straight through your system without any nutritional benefit to you. So it is vitally important to thoroughly chew your food. The old saying of chewing your food 16 times before swallowing has a lot of merit.

Before you eat you must be physically hungry. If you are not hungry, your mind will be the one making the decision, not your body. Since it is your body that you are feeding, it is important to listen to the clues it gives you. The more accurate a match you make between your hunger and the foods you eat, the less you will eat. Are you frightened that you may eat too much, that your hunger is bottomless? Don't be. Years of dieting and suppressing your appetite have made you not trust the very thing that is the key to successful weight loss.

Master your hunger

Your hunger will always start off softly. Don't give into it in the early stages, as often this is your habitual or clock hunger. Wait at least 30 minutes after the first signal before you feed your body. Observe where your hunger is coming from. Is it in your stomach, abdomen, mouth? How does it feel to be hungry like this? When I am hungry I start to feel an emptiness in my stomach, which then starts to squirm. My hunger growls and becomes louder, rising from my abdomen to my stomach, up to my throat. I salivate more.

Feed your body with what it wants. It knows best what you need to keep your energy going. Maybe this is bread, pasta, fruit. Listen to it. Don't be sidetracked by alluring external factors. Close your eyes, listen, feel, taste and visualise exactly what it is your hunger wants. Don't judge. You will know when you have listened correctly and, amazingly, you will find that what your body wanted was just what you needed. Food will satisfy you in ways you have never experienced. Food satisfies you physically as well as emotionally, and when you listen to your Inner Wisdom, this will take care of the two. A great example of this is when we feel a bit sick and sorry for ourselves. All we want to eat is a big bowl of homemade soup, just like mum used to make. And it works!

Get to know your hunger intimately

Right now I am not hungry at all. I have been very satisfied with light meals today, as I ate quite heavily the day before. My hunger is sleeping quietly and wants my appetite to do the same. I honour my body and respect its decisions unquestioningly.

Exercise
1. Over the next week, rate your hunger roar before you eat on a scale of one to five, one being a soft purr and five being a huge roar. Observe how much in sync you are with your hunger. You will be quite surprised at the results. Often the results are very different from what was expected. Start to get into the habit of

mentally rating your hunger. This will help you become more aware of just how hungry you are when you decide to eat.

2. Don't eat at your regular meal times for a few days. If, say, you always have breakfast as soon as you wake up, try not to eat until you experience tummy grumbles. Watch and observe. Do you anticipate hunger, wanting it to come soon so that you can eat?

3. Eat by your body clock hunger. When you start eating by listening to your body clock, all other clocks must go out the window. This may be difficult if you have a scheduled eating time, for when you start listening to your body hunger, in the beginning it may want to eat at the most awkward times. I believe it is far better to wait until you are hungry to eat, rather than store up for anticipated hunger. You can bring a snack box to work and eat at morning tea to stave off the really loud hunger calls.

4. Try going without lunch in your lunch break and notice if you feel deprived or not. Then go a day without eating dinner. Just sit with your family and have a cup of tea. How do you feel? Deprived, stupid, annoyed?

5. Eat when you are not hungry — this one shouldn't be too difficult. Write down what food you chose, how it tasted, how you felt, and how much you ate.

It is important that you learn to differentiate between physical hunger and all the other types of hunger. If you eat purely out of physical hunger, it certainly cuts out a lot of other eating. The problem is, if you cut out all the times you eat, bar when you eat from physical hunger, there is a huge gap. What do you put in its place? Because you have used food for many different emotional hunger reasons, it does take some time and working on yourself to get to the stage of eating always out of physical hunger. We will discuss emotional eating in more detail in the next part of the book.

It is a great feeling of control to be able to eat when you are hungry, but we are not super humans. There will be times when you will eat when you are not hungry. People with normal weight do this, too — just watch them.

A perfect example of this was an incident this morning. Kev said to me, "I really don't feel like eating this time of the morning — 6.30 am is a bit early for me". I said, "Well, why are you eating?" He replied: "I am eating to gain some energy. I am having a few spoonfuls of high-powered food to keep me going." This is the response of someone who doesn't have a weight problem. Just a few spoonfuls of food was enough for him, mentally and physically. There are always times when people eat when they are not really hungry. The difference is that those of us who have a weight problem seem to do so far more frequently! We need to explore our non-physical hungers and find out what we are really hungry for.

Know your other hungers
When I first started following my hunger, I was quite shocked to find I rarely, if ever, ate for physical hunger. There were too many other reasons to eat. I have listed some of them below. Tick the ones that relate to you.

Social hunger
"I'm not really hungry, but mealtimes are the only times the family gets together." Eating together is important, especially if you are from a European family. Imagine sitting at the table and saying "I am not hungry, but I just want to sit here and be with you all." Would you get a few surprised looks? Or would your family think you were on another crazy diet, the 'don't-eat-at-mealtimes' diet?

Clock hunger
You look at your watch and it is 12.30 pm. You say to yourself "Oh, I must be hungry, it's 12.30". Clock hunger is habitual, and we have mastered the art of manipulating our minds to believe we will be hungry at certain times. Stop wearing watches and looking at external clocks, and start listening to your internal clock.

Mouth hunger
"I really need to shove some food into my mouth, even though I am not hungry." You know this game: stuff in as much as you can.

Future hunger
I love this one: "I'm not really hungry now, but it will be two hours before I get a chance to eat, so I'd better have something now."

Nervous hunger
"I just have to eat something now. What can I cram into my mouth?"

Boredom hunger
"I'm not in the mood to do anything. Eating sounds good."

I deserve food
"I've had such a terrible day. I need some chocolate to cheer me up."

Food = guaranteed pleasure
"Eating treats is the only way I know how to cheer myself up", or "I have had such a great day — let's eat to celebrate".

Doing thankless jobs for others
Being a woman, wife, mother, carer, friend and helper is very demanding work: "I look after everyone else; food is my reward for being a helper".

Anger hunger
Most of us are not taught to deal with anger in a constructive way. We don't know what to say or how to say it, and if we start to express how we feel, quite often we get labelled 'over-emotional' or 'hysterical'. So we say to ourselves: "It's easier to swallow my anger with food than to express it".

How many of the 'hungers' did you tick? Quite a few, I imagine — if you were being honest with yourself. Imagine if you ate only out of physical hunger. Just think of how much other eating would be cut out! This frightens many of us — after all, if you have seldom eaten for physical hunger, how do you know what it is, and what will you do with all those non-physical eating episodes?

Master your hunger — beliefs that have to go
Let me help you overcome some of the most common fears I have encountered.

1. "If I let myself eat when I am hungry, I won't be able to stop eating."
Let's face it: after however many years of dieting, not listening to your hunger and denying it food, your hunger is going to be like a bull at a gate, itching and snorting and puffing to get out and experience life on the other side, with all its freedom. It is angry for being cooped up for so long. We are led to believe our hunger is an untamable beast who doesn't know the meaning of the word 'stop', but in reality the opposite is true. Your hunger has the roar of a lion, but if you stay in touch with it after feeding it what it really wants, it will be a subdued kitten. Trust and patience will win through. Eating when you are physically hungry is an extremely rewarding and empowering experience. A friend at work said to me the other day that his motto for eating is, 'Never eat more than you can lift'. At the end of the day, a sense of humour will always get you through.

2. "I won't be able to eat as much if I only eat when I am physically hungry."
Often the amount of food you think you want is not as much as your body wants. The old saying, 'your eyes are bigger than your belly', does have truth to it. One Easter I wanted to eat a roomfull of Easter eggs and, what's more, I believed I could! Halfway through my second egg, my body said, "please stop; I don't want any more", yet my mind said, "let's finish the whole lot".

However, I had learnt that listening to my Inner Wisdom was the key, and I stopped at two eggs. Check your thoughts every time you turn to food when you are not hungry. They will indicate to you that you want something less tangible and that you may not be able to get it there and then. If you are upset, you may just want a great big hug, but you turn to ice-cream instead.

You must make yourself aware that you are reaching for food and direct your thoughts to the food by asking it what you want it to do for you and how you want it to make you feel. If you could turn the food into anything, what would it be? A hug? A cuddle? What are you needing badly in your life that food is being made a substitute for? Our hungers can be endless, and if we do not satisfy these hungers in other ways, the more we will eat to stop these feelings.

I remember many times that I felt I could have devoured the whole world, and a plate of food felt like an entree. No amount of food would or could satisfy me. Our bottomless hunger indicates that there is a hole in our life that needs to be filled. What do you need filled in your life right now? More love, fun, happiness, energy, time out? Is there an imbalance, with too much stress, work or not enough time out for yourself? As I have stressed, I see many women who use food as their 'time out' because they don't feel they are worthy to have time out, or they feel guilty for being too self-indulgent as so many people are depending on them for other things. All women I talk to want more time out. Caring for other's needs leaves them exhausted and resentful. You must make time out for yourself if you are to be happy on the inside and outside.

A lot of unnecessary eating is done to compensate for not nurturing yourself when you need time out. This doesn't help the situation at all. No matter what your situation is in life right now, you can afford at least 15 minutes time out every day. At the very least, stick a note on the bathroom door that reads 'Do Not Disturb' and be very loyal to yourself about doing this. Much is gained from a small time-out session.

3. "If good food is around when I am not physically hungry, I may not get a chance to eat some."

The fear of missing out can be very strong, especially if the food is special — those golden goodies you seldom get a chance to eat. I remember on many social occasions stuffing myself with every food I could get my hands on and eating it quickly, getting away with not too many people noticing. I didn't want to miss that taste sensation — it was like a drug. Devouring chocolate mouse was nearly as good as sex, and I wasn't for the life of me going to miss that sensation. BUT eating when you are not hungry comes with a high price, especially in the 'taking care of yourself' stakes — the feeling of complete lack of control, the physically sick feeling and the self-hate.

You always have the option of taking some food home, or buying something exactly like it the next day. But do not give yourself a hard time when you eat out of emotional hunger — you're starting something new and it will take time to change. Sometimes you will not have a clue why you eat when you are not hungry — that's okay, too. Just work on the more obvious situations. When we reach for food too quickly, we do not let any true feelings or emotions surface because we stifle them with food and just concentrate on the issue of being fat and having no self-control. There are so many reasons we turn to food when we are not hungry. It can be a mixture of many issues and emotions. Work at your own pace. I used to work on one issue a day. Sometimes I would get very frustrated and think, "I don't know what is going on, I just want to eat". Take time, be patient and take small steps. When you begin to see that your physical hungers can be fulfilled, you can start to realise that there is the same possibility for all your emotional hungers.

HANDY HINTS

CUT DOWN ON THE NON-PHYSICAL REASONS YOU EAT.
GET TO KNOW YOUR OWN HUNGER AS A FRIEND.
DO YOUR HUNGER LEVEL CHECKS WHENEVER YOU EAT.
HAVE A DAILY 'TIME-OUT' PERIOD FOR YOURSELF AND TREAT IT SACREDLY.

CHAPTER FIFTEEN

HOW TO EAT
WHAT YOU WANT AND ENJOY IT

Success step 2: Eat foods you really like.
Dieter's belief: Eating what I really want will make me fat.

At first, people are usually very suspicious of this success step. To many of us, eating what you want means eating everything! Chocolate, cake, ice-cream, chips — you name it, you will want it. "How can I possibly lose weight eating all this?" I hear you ask. Now let's not be too hard on ourselves. Think of all the years you have been dieting. It's as though now you've been let out of jail. You go crazy for a while, making up for all those times you couldn't eat what you wanted. Again, in comes trust, patience and kindness to yourself. Believe me when I say that the novelty does wear off much more quickly than you think. Remember, people who don't have a weight problem eat what they want, not giving food a second thought.

Eating what we want is quite foreign to most of us. Throughout our lives we have been told by the diet industry, magazines, television, mothers, fathers, husbands, wives, friends, boyfriends and girlfriends, what we should and should not eat. Somewhere along the way we gave away our control. Many women find it difficult to decide what it is that they really want because the decision is still shrouded in a judgmental voice.

To me eating what I really want means going for the double, choc-chip, full cream ice-cream, knowing that the low-calorie ice confectionery with liquid sauce just will not do. You see, you cannot trick yourself by going for the low-calorie version, thinking that it will satisfy you. What usually happens is that you will feel unsatisfied and will eat everything around the desired food, finally eating it with guilt, not enjoying the taste at all. That is called 'taking the long road' and it isn't worth the effort! By being true to yourself and eating the foods you really want, you will satisfy yourself emotionally and physically, and the need to go searching further greatly diminishes.

I remember many times thinking how good and disciplined I was for resisting my urges to eat 'bad foods', eating salad and dry toast instead of mayonnaise and buttered toast. But by the end of the day I would get bored playing that game, and I would go for the crackers with low-calorie spread. Still that wouldn't do, so I would go on to the next phase, which was another dieter's mind-set: 'eat anything, but no sweets'. That game wore off after a while, so on I went to the next phase: one sweet biscuit. That game wore off very quickly and so did all the rules. Then it was open slather: 'eat anything and everything as quickly as you can'. This game never had any winners, only a miserable, bloated loser.

It is important to remember that you can't go back and eat for all the times you've felt deprived in some way. There just isn't enough food around to fill the voids created by the ways you deprive yourself on both a physical and emotional level. You may find that your desire for tantalising, delicious food is endless. But a trust in yourself will develop as your Inner Wisdom guides you to your needed choices as opposed to having no choices at all.

If you let yourself really eat what you want, the magic of having it wears off. Once you know you can have that food any time you want, you will settle down and get on with eating other foods. Start to enjoy your heart's desires. If a hot chocolate is what you want, nothing but full cream milk with cream and marshmallows will do.

By this stage you may be salivating at the mouth, thinking of the hundreds of different foods you want to lay your hands on. Then all of a sudden a little voice says, "Hey, hold on, if you eat what you really like, you are not going to lose weight. You are going to get fatter than you have ever been." You might be starting to feel scared, panicky, suspicious, and a bit excited as well.

You will always feel a mixture of being scared and relieved, with a dash of suspicion. Your thoughts will be something like: "I feel relieved to eat what I want, but I am scared I will keep eating, and I feel suspicious of how I am going to lose weight doing this. After all, look what happens when I'm not in control of my eating: I get fat." These kinds of thoughts and the feelings that go with them are common responses. This dieter's belief of not being able to lose weight without dieting is very deeply embedded. It is reaffirmed all the time by the diet industry telling us that we need them to control our weight because we can't control it ourselves. Otherwise we wouldn't be so overweight. Be very aware of the subtle and not so subtle ways you are being told that you are the one with the problem. The opposite is true. Don't get sucked into this mind-set any more. Stop right now and take a minute to think of all the other millions of people in this world who eat what they want and still remain at a balanced weight.

Because we are so obsessed with our weight, we tend to magnify our problem and see it as an impenetrable barrier around us. Trust your body's intelligence. Our wisest teacher, the one within us, knows. So don't stifle it any more. Trust your choices. For a while you will want to make up for all the years of deprivation and you may find yourself eating as though you are on one giant binge. There is not much you can do about this, so just let it happen and accept it. It is a natural repercussion of denying yourself food. You must go through it to get to the other side. Soon enough you will want to get back on track, eating foods that make you feel full of vitality and give you a body that matches.

The more you eat what you really want, the less fear you will have

The more you eat what you truly want, the less fear you will have. It takes a while but gradually, over time, you will tune in with your body's wisdom and honour its choices, which will be right for you. You will feel great that you are listening to your Inner Wisdom, and things will start getting easier. After a while you will do what you always thought was impossible: you will leave some of your favourite food on your plate! When you realise you can eat any food you want, the need and desire to have all food, all the time, disappears — foods become ordinary.

What food is right for me? Whom should I listen to?

All I am going to say about what type of food is right for you is this: if after you have eaten a meal, you feel physically nourished, light, energetic, mentally alert, content and happy, then that food is right for you. If you feel dull, heavy, lethargic, bloated, then that food or the combination of foods you ate, isn't right for you. There are millions of books that so-called experts have written about the way to ultimate health through diet and nutrition. They are all pushing their own barrow to ultimate health. What I know is that whatever they have written is right for them, but it may not be right for you. Don't get me wrong — some health experts make very valid and important points about health and nutrition. There is a lot to be said for eating food in its most pure and unrefined state. That to me is common sense. But don't deny your urges to experiment and try other foods. You are too delicate from diet deprivation to be following any stringent rules.

How do I know what I really want to eat? — Powerful tools to help you

1. If you listen to your body and ask yourself what it is you really want to eat, in your mind you will conjure up a tasty feast and you will instantly know what it is you want. This vision is so real that you can taste and smell the food. And it is very definite, such as mashed potato with mushrooms and gravy, and nothing

else will do. Sometimes you will find that this feast will take preparation, but that is okay. You won't mind the preparation because you know how much you are going to enjoy it. These internal food choices satisfy you emotionally and physically because they are right for you at the time. When you eat these foods they satisfy you both physically and mentally, and you do not go hunting for more food fifteen minutes later. After eating you forget about food and get along with the next thing in your day. Yes, it is true — you forget about food, like all those other 'ordinary' people. You become like them.

If you do not listen to your body's choices and go for an external food choice, you will suffer the consequences of feeling dissatisfied physically and/or mentally with your food choices. Generally these external choices are when you choose foods that you did not want till they saw you! They curled their finger at you, beckoning you to eat them. External food choices usually involve the bakery kind or the ones at the supermarket check-out. These foods are quick and ready to eat. They are difficult to stop eating because the desire for them originated externally. You saw and smelt the food, and if your Inner Wisdom did not want you to start eating, it sure enough will not know how to stop you.

We eat 'external foods' most of the time. Advertising makes sure of that. Don't you just loathe magazines that have a chocolate bar blown up 300 per cent on one page and a new diet for summer on the next? Where is the fairness in that!

Remember, your aim is to honour your Internal Wisdom which knows best.

2. For one week make a note of where your eating desires and food choices came from. Divide your page into two, with the heading Internal Cue on one side and External Cue on the other. If you write foods in the external column, make sure you note where the cue came from: for example, walking past a bakery, supermarket aisle, etc. This is a very enlightening exercise. You will find it extremely rewarding to do as you will discover so much more about your eating habits and patterns.

3. Don't feel bad about admitting you do not want to eat the food you have prepared or bought. We can't be on cue all the time. Sometimes other thoughts and desires get in the way. When this happens, be prepared to store the food and get yourself something else. Vow to yourself that at the next meal you will really find the food you want. If you are with other people, it is okay to say, "I don't really feel like this", and get something else you would prefer to eat. Also, try not to pre-plan too far in advance. At 9.00 am in the morning you may think you want pasta and chicken for your evening meal, but by the time your evening mealtime comes around, you may feel like fish and salad. Plan as close as is practical to your actual mealtime.

Some women will go to great lengths to get the food they really want. I know of a lady who drives 20 kilometres to the best fish and chip shop in town, as nothing else will do for her. You may go through stages like this. Why settle for second best? But be realistic. We cannot fly to Italy every time we want the best pizza. Sometimes we have to settle for that which is most convenient.

4. It is also a good idea to sit for a minute or two before eating and get in touch with your hunger and ask it what it wants to feed you. Place your hands on your stomach and ask yourself: "What food do I want to eat to nourish me right now?" Wait for a picture to come up. If this doesn't happen, go deeper and ask yourself whether you want something spicy, sweet or plain, something hot, cold or at room temperature, something crunchy, soft or hard. This will help you focus on what it is you want. If you still are unsure, ask yourself if your hunger roar is loud enough to warrant eating right now. Finding the perfect match between your hunger and the food you want can be quite difficult. You need to test a variety of foods in your imagination to identify what it is you want. Go beyond your taste buds and imagine what the food would taste like in your stomach.

5. Discover your likes and dislikes. By answering the following simple questions you will gain a good understanding of your food preferences. It is not until you see your answers down on

paper that you really get the full picture, so write them down. What foods do I like? Why do I like these foods? How do these foods make me feel, physically and emotionally, after eating them? What foods don't I like? Why don't I like these foods? How do these foods make me feel, physically and emotionally, after eating them?

6. Squash excuses that stem from dieter's mind-set such as, "I can't afford to really eat what I want". "I can't afford to eat what I want" means "I don't want to spend money and treat myself" or "I can't eat foods that are forbidden". If you go for top-quality chocolate, paté, dried tomatoes or whatever it is you desire as soon as you want these foods, you will probably end up saving yourself time and money. How many times have you refrained from buying yourself food at the supermarket, only to buy it at double the price at your local store? Just think how much money you have spent on diet foods. One of my workshop participants said that the only reason she didn't go back to diet-packaged food and a program was because she couldn't afford the $800.00 it would end up costing her. Now $800.00 can buy a lot of delicious food. This lady is presently very glad she came along to my workshop!

Another common excuse is, "It's too hard for me to eat what I want". A solution is to have a snack box containing all the foods you like, which you can readily eat if you desire. I get a lot of laughter from women when I tell them to get a snack box. They have visualisations of children going to school with their plastic lunch boxes. Think about it: you pack lunches for other family members, so why not for yourself? Take the time to think about what you want. Don't you deserve time for yourself? By carrying this food around with you, you are announcing your need to eat and your snack box is tangible proof of that. You are telling yourself and others that you have needs and that you will meet those needs. You are saying that you no longer value staving off hunger until someone else's pre-determined mealtime.

HANDY HINTS

Make an effort to eat foods that your Inner Wisdom chooses.

Use the questioning technique before you decide what to eat.

Try not to pre-plan meals too far in advance.

CHAPTER SIXTEEN

ENJOY THE ATMOSPHERE
AND ABUNDANCE OF FOOD

Success step 3: Provide yourself with a great selection of foods.
Dieter's belief: I only eat the foods I know are legal.

This is another belief you need to break away from. Once you work on the step of eating what you really want, then start to expand your food choices. Go now and have a look in your kitchen cupboards and fridge. What sort of foods do you find there? Is it a rather pathetic picture, like old Mother Hubbard's cupboards? If I asked you to go to the supermarket and fill your trolley up with food, what sort of food would be in there? Are you stuck in a rut with your choices? By answering these questions, you will be able to gauge how much you need to work on yourself to feel comfortable around an abundance of all types of food.

If you are having difficulty bringing in a variety and abundance of food, what are the reasons for this? Were you brought up to be thrifty with food? If this is this case, you will then tend to come up with all sorts of reasons for not bringing food into the house, such as, "I have every type of food I need at my finger-tips, just around the corner in the Deli" or, "If I have it, I will eat it". The fact is, if the food isn't within reach when you want it, the legalising process will not work. Creating a distance between you and the food you really want when you are hungry will end up, usually, with overeating. If you don't have food in the house and don't feel like going to the local shop, what will you do? You will probably overeat on whatever is available in the house; like a ferret you will sniff out every nook and cranny in an effort to find some kind of satisfaction for your craving. If you don't take the trouble to go out for the food you want, you will, more than likely, eat more than you really want.

Now is the time to break free and indulge your senses in the wonderful variety of food that we are fortunate to have in this country. You know those food suggestions on packets that you always thought looked nice? Well, try them out! Dare to be different. Sample foods from all over the world. Go to the markets and try fresh foods and exotic foods — as much as your budget will allow. Take the time to prepare a satisfying meal that you enjoy. This will register deeply in your subconscious that you really do care for your well-being. A satisfying meal will also keep you physically satisfied for a lot longer than if you just snack. The need to go out grazing for more will greatly diminish. Having a meal that satisfies you for a few hours will give you time to concentrate on other things.

You may be wondering what exactly makes a satisfying meal? You will probably eat many different combinations and types of food to make up for the deprivation years, but after a while your Inner Wisdom will want to nourish your body with satisfying meals, using a lovely selection of foods. But only you can determine what is the right combination for you. Experiment with different types of foods and make every meal as appetising as you can.

Success step 4: Sit and eat slowly, in a calming atmosphere.

Dieter's belief: Sitting down and enjoying food is only for thin people.

How much of your eating is done sitting down (and eating in the car doesn't count)? Make a list of the places where you eat. I will get the ball rolling and you can add to the list: in the car, at the fridge, on the bus/train, at the sink ...

Why don't you give yourself time to sit down and eat? Is it because you feel it is not important to you, that you can't afford the time? Do you feel that enjoying eating will make you want to eat more and will make you fatter? Why can't you, or why don't you, want to sit and eat? We have this belief that it is okay to eat a salad sitting down, but not a bar of chocolate — that has to be done quickly without being too aware. When you are in conflict with your weight, you believe you do not deserve to eat like a 'normal' person, sitting down. You don't believe you are allowed to enjoy food because you are fat and have overindulged anyway.

You *must* take time out and enjoy your food; life is too short. Try it just for one meal a day and work up from there. The more times you sit and eat with awareness, the more satisfied you will be as you are taking care of yourself physically and emotionally.

Your body likes to really nourish you in a calm atmosphere. Watch animals — they don't like anyone hanging around when they eat. They will go to the quietest place available and eat sitting in a comfortable position. After eating they will laze around, relishing their dinner and, most probably, will have a snooze. It baffles me how people can eat walking in a crowded street. It is stressful enough just walking in a crowd, let alone eating as well. If you are not calm when you eat, your stomach becomes tense and knotted and indigestion will result.

Atmosphere and the art of concentration
How much mindless eating do you do in front of the TV or whilst reading the paper? "I reached to grab a chip and they were all gone; I don't know where they went" is a phrase commonly used by the diet fraternity. When we are doing other things besides eating, it is hard to know when to stop, as we are not focusing fully on eating. We are not listening to our stomach when it says, "I've had enough, thank you. Can we please stop now?" How much of your eating time is spent doing other things, too?

Can you remember the last time you sat down to eat and did nothing else but enjoy your food? We are usually doing the exact opposite, grabbing a bite to eat on the run and thinking of all the other things we should be doing. Not paying attention to and enjoying food, more often than not, results in overeating as we are hardly aware of what we have eaten, let alone how much! By denying yourself time out to eat, you are subconsciously telling yourself that you are not worthy of taking time out and that you are bad in some way.

Here's a way to really get into the swing of enjoying eating. Choose a time when you can eat alone. Then set the table, taking take out your best crockery, cutlery, tablecloth and napkins. Put some flowers or a candle on the table. Bring out your favorite food and enjoy.

Discover the real art of eating awareness

Get yourself one sultana. Study it, roll it around with your fingers, feeling the texture. Think how it came to be a sultana. Look at its shape. Now pop it into your mouth and close your eyes. Roll it around your mouth. Feel the texture with your tongue. Observe your anticipation to eat it, with an increase in saliva in your mouth. Now bite into it once. Feel it burst and taste the new flavour, the new texture. Keep biting and chewing until it is finely masticated, and then swallow. That is what I call eating with maximum awareness and concentration! When you eat slowly and with full concentration, you will notice that food tastes so much better and a little tends to satisfy you. Try sucking one piece of chocolate and not biting into it. You will find one piece goes a long way. You may realise that some foods taste much nicer than you thought or some don't taste as good as you thought they did. One of my workshop participants said: "Eating chocolate that slow made me become aware of the texture and fullness, its creaminess and thickness. I was amazed just how satisfying one piece could be."

Be in the present moment and do not think ahead

This is easier said than done, as most of us are thinking 'dessert' while eating our main meal or thinking of what chores need to be done. I used to think that food tasted better in my mind than in my mouth. When I was just thinking about food I would imagine how delicious it would be, but when I actually ate it I was too busy thinking that I shouldn't be eating it and I kept my mind distracted by thinking what I needed to do next. Sound familiar?

Non-awareness eating
Here are some more wonderful ways we eat while trying to believe that we are not really eating: eating thin or odd slices of cake to tidy up the shape of a cake, cutting super thin slices of a food, eating free samples at the supermarket, eating scraps and leftovers, eating on the run, sampling food by licking spoons, sampling food when cooking ...

This type of non-awareness eating becomes a bit of a game to us. I must admit, I do like the free samples at the supermarket, but I view it as fun, not as an opportunity to grab as much as I can. Eating this way will not satisfy you because your mind is elsewhere. You feel guilty eating more than you should, so you switch your mind to 'not here'. That way you can be oblivious to what and how much you are eating and the guilt feelings that go with it. But you deserve better than this, don't you? To see how absurd it really is, picture a scene where you invite a group of friends over for dinner. Upon arrival at your house you tell them entree is leftovers, main course consists of a few spoonfuls of supermarket samples as well as licking from spoons used to cook with, and dessert will take place at the bakery sampler section! Quite a humorous scene, isn't it!

Eat in full view of other people
A friend of mine once said to me that she found it really difficult to eat in front of other work colleagues because they always ate 'diet' foods and were thinner. She felt they ridiculed her eating 'non-diet' food: "I really wanted a hamburger and a milk drink the other day and I decided to eat in front of the other staff. All they did was make smart comments about what would have been better for me to eat. I didn't enjoy my lunch at all." We all go

through experiences like this one and it takes courage to say: "I've had enough misery, eating foods I don't want or like, hiding and feeling like some criminal. I'm not going to play this game any more."

If you are not sure what approach to take, here are a few tips. Tell work-mates, family or friends: "Look, I would appreciate it if you didn't tell me what I should and shouldn't eat. I'm not into this diet scene any more. I'm doing my own thing." Or just go and find a nice, quiet place on your own and enjoy being with yourself for a while. Remember, eating is a form of meditation; and in meditation, concentration and focus on what you are doing are the key.

Why should we eat what others think we should? We are taking care of ourselves first and that means being true to our cause. We do not have to prove to the world around us that we really are good people, trying to lose weight by eating chicken with no skin, salad with no dressing, lo-cal this and that. That is just degrading yourself; it is like saying: "Look at me, please like me even though I'm fat. I am trying to do something about it." We do not need anyone else's approval. This takes courage and the belief that we are allowed to enjoy food. It is not a crime being fat and really eating what you want in public. Find a group of weight-conscious females, and sit close by with the biggest, most wicked piece of chocolate cake and eat it in the loudest, most enjoyable way possible.

HANDY HINTS

CREATE THE BEST ATMOSPHERE YOU CAN WHEN YOU EAT.
ALWAYS SIT DOWN TO EAT ANY TYPE AND AMOUNT OF FOOD.
EAT ALL FOODS IN FULL VIEW OF OTHERS.

CHAPTER SEVENTEEN

KNOWING WHEN TO STOP —
MASTERING SATISFACTION

Dieter's belief: I only know two settings: full and more full.
Success step 5: Stop eating when you are satisfied.

Most of us are a little bit rusty in the art of satisfaction, due to complete lack of use. So many layers of other emotions waiting to be satisfied have pushed our intuitive voice of food-satisfaction deep down. But don't worry — your body will always tell you when enough is enough if you tune in and listen. You will be truly amazed how clear it really is.

We are going to learn to master satisfaction. Success with this eating step is most important. It will lead you to the home stretch and will give you a wonderful feeling of self-empowerment. But don't give yourself a hard time by trying to get there too quickly. After all the years of deprivation, your body will want to be oversatisfied for a little while, but when it realises you will feed it when it is hungry, and that you will feed it what it wants, it will begin to relax and want less food.

When is enough, enough? How do you know when you should physically stop eating? I remember many eating episodes where I ended up with a drum-tight belly, having to undo my buttons or belt. Many women do not believe they have a voice that tells them to stop eating. They cling onto old, ingrained beliefs such as, "It takes 20 minutes to register in the brain that it has been fed" or, "My stomach is so stretched it can't be relied upon". I don't believe these theories and neither should you. They are a cop-out and will not help you in any way.

When you decide to stop eating depends on why you are eating in the first place. If you eat out of boredom and you are a very bored person, you could be eating for a very long time. Throw in a bit of guilt and you might keep on going until you have eaten everything in sight. When your mind is focused on the judgments and not on the food, it is difficult to know when to stop eating.

So the secret is first to observe whether you are eating for physical hunger — if your tummy isn't rumbling and growling, then it isn't physical hunger. The next step is to decide what type of hunger you have. If you can't define it, just gauge the strength of it. If it's very strong it usually indicates a strong emotion/feeling or situation you suppress frequently.

Satisfaction is relative to your moods, your emotional needs and physical well-being. When I was sick as a child, my mother used to feed me soup and soldier toast. It satisfied me physically and emotionally, and the same can be said in my adult life. Sometimes if I am feeling down, warm soups and hot foods satisfy me physically and emotionally. One day is different from the next. Do not place strict rules on satisfaction. For example, the belief that you 'must have a balanced meal or else you will not be satisfied' will only lead to further unnecessary eating.

It is important to understand why you can't stop eating, even though you have had enough. Picture this scene: you are in the middle of enjoying a beautiful dinner. Mmm, the food tastes so good! You close your eyes, wanting to savour the flavour forever. It is hard to give up the delicious taste of food in your mouth, that wonderful taste that is like a drug, leaving you wanting more and more. You keep on eating and eating, past your satisfaction level. As you begin to pay attention to your eating, all of a sudden you notice that the delicious taste has quickly

KNOWING WHEN TO STOP — MASTERING SATISFACTION

diminished and, very soon, you can't even stand the sight of food.

How many times can you remember wanting to hold onto a 'delicious taste moment' even after you were feeling full? It is hard to let go sometimes. If someone asked you to put down your knife and fork in one of these moments, it would appear an impossible request. What is really going on is a subconscious delay tactic of not wanting to return to reality, to bury deeper the feelings that we don't want surfacing. When we are in the delicious food moment, all other thoughts temporarily float off into oblivion and the taste sensation is all we care about. When you feel yourself stuck in the delicious taste moment, ask yourself: "Do I really need to lose myself in the food, or can I allow the sensation to pass and leave me with my feelings?" As you learn to accept and respect your feelings of fullness, you will find that where you previously couldn't even get up from the table, you are now at a more comfortable level of satisfaction. The trick is to listen to your intuition, which will tell you when enough is enough, and to become able to leave the table, feeling a sense of satisfaction and self-empowerment.

If you get a lot of enjoyment from eating even after you have had enough, there needs to be something equally enjoyable about putting down your knife and fork, other than just doing the dishes. Remember back to your childhood when you couldn't wait to finish a meal so you could go out and play again? You need to have that same kind of feeling again. Don't do any activity that leaves you hanging around the kitchen for too long. Doing something fun and enjoyable straight after dinner will help enormously to divert your attention from food. You will be rewarded with an enormous sense of satisfaction, knowing that you, rather than the food, are in control.

As you let yourself eat all food and begin to use it as fuel, it will start to lose some of its magical power, as we have pointed out. But remember, food still has the potential to be a magical soother of pain if you don't make a conscious effort to rid yourself of this hold it can have over you. You must also be willing to say to yourself that you have had enough food to satisfy you, that food can satisfy only what it is meant to, and you must feel comfortable saying, "No more, thanks, I'm satisfied".

Mastery techniques for stopping eating at the satisfaction level

1. Allow sufficient quantities of foods in your house — more than you could possibly eat at the one time. If you feel like a biscuit, make sure your biscuit jar is full. If you eat ice-cream, make sure you have buckets of it in the freezer. If you are cooking lasagna, make sure you have ample spaghetti and sauce left over. Having surplus will relax you. Surplus will remind you that you can have whatever you want, whenever you want. Deciding your own portions instead of buying pre-portioned food, which is someone else's idea about the 'right' portion, can help you, too.

2. Get to know the difference between feeling that you *must* stop eating when you are feeling full and feeling that you would *like* to stop eating. A sure route to failure is using words like 'must'. Change these strict words to 'choose' and 'like'. Soon enough you will start to recognise who you are as an eater. Being able to stop eating when you are satisfied goes hand in hand with eating when you are physically hungry and eating what you want. All of these components strengthen your sense of security and lessen your need to use food as magic.

3. You need to discover other ways than food to satisfy the areas of your life that are not getting proper attention, such as emotional support, love, comfort, and time out for yourself. If your life is filled up with a lot of unsatisfied areas, then it is going to be difficult to say "I'm satisfied" after eating. Women in my workshops are often shocked when they discover how little food they really need, but also disturbed by this discovery. There is the thought of "Oh, I cannot stop eating when around food, my hunger is bottomless" and the revelation that they can be satisfied with only small portions. The two don't seem compatible. When you start seeing food as simply food, you do not need very much of it. On the other hand, when you use food to express how needy you feel and how bad you feel about needing so much, no portion

KNOWING WHEN TO STOP — MASTERING SATISFACTION

of food is ever big enough to fill that void. When you think it is more important to gauge the level of fullness or emptiness in your stomach rather than the fullness or emptiness of your plate, you are starting to gain control. The good feeling that comes from respecting your Inner Wisdom and the personal power that comes from following it will eventually replace the false sense of eating more food than you need.

4. Don't turn eating what you want into a diet or a restricted eating routine. When you start eating what you want and you stop when you are satisfied, weight loss is inevitable. Be sure not to turn this 'stop when I've had enough' into a control routine with rules, for the Rebel from your diet days will surely rear its ugly head again with all its strict rules.

5. To help you understand your satisfaction levels, visualise a fuel guage whenever you decide to eat, and rate your level of satisfaction. Remember, awareness is the key.

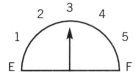

Level one
Your stomach is empty; some growling and gurgling may occur; there is no feeling of food in your system from previous meals. This is the point at which you should start eating.

Level two
You feel physically hungry. If you stop eating at this stage, you ward off hunger pangs.

Level three
This is the level of maximum comfort. You feel completely satisfied, with no sensation of hunger and no discomfort from overeating. This is the level at which you should stop eating. This is about three-quarters of your stomach's capacity for eating.

Level four
You have gone past your stomach's comfort level and feel some bloating, heaviness, lethargy, and dullness in your stomach, and you loosen your clothing. (You will be frequently at this level in the beginning.)

Level five
You are well and truly stuffed. All you want to do is lie down and go to sleep.

6. Practice getting to know different satisfaction levels.
   (a) Leave half your dinner on your plate and then rate your level of satisfaction. How does it feel to leave half of your meal on the plate?
   (b) When you are in the middle of a meal, put your knife and fork down. This can be very difficult, for once the cutlery starts moving, sparks fly and it is hard to stop the hand-to-mouth momentum. But do it, and go into another room if you have to. Come back and reassess your satisfaction level.
   (c) Push your plate away with food still on it. Do this once a day for one week.
   (d) Concentrate on the delicious taste feelings you have with food. Notice the subtle shift in your thinking from enjoying the food's taste to the urgency or desire to eat all you can while you can. This shift usually happens after you are physically satisfied but before all the food is gone. What type of messages do you give yourself? How is your self-image after your satisfaction climbs over level four? Do you have fears about not getting enough food?
   (e) If I told you that you could have whatever food you wanted, any time, would you still be eating? When are you prepared to stop eating and say, "I want to feel good and take care of myself"? The decision to feel satisfied and happy or stuffed and unhappy after a meal is entirely in your hands.

KNOWING WHEN TO STOP — MASTERING SATISFACTION

A special word on the 'clean-the-plate club'
Dieter's belief: I must eat everything on my plate before I can have dessert.

The desire to eat everything on your plate is also probably fuelled by your belief in the club. You are one member who keeps the club going through the generations. Remember back to your childhood, being told "you must eat all that's on your plate; think of all the starving children" or, "eat all your vegies or you will get no dessert". Can you remember all the tricks of trying to get away with not eating the foods you didn't like? Like putting them under the table, under the plate, or giving them to the dog?

Holding onto the 'clean-the-plate' belief is absolutely crazy. Just try to picture sending your leftovers to all the starving children in India. It would not pass through customs. If it did, think what state it would be in by the time it arrived. Not even a starving child would want to eat it. Because these beliefs have been instilled in us for such a long time, we hold on to them dearly. How many of you are mothers guilty of telling your children to eat everything on their plate? Yes, it seems to pass down through the generations. We live in good times. Many of our parents went through tough times in the depression or war years. So we have this in-built mentality that if food is put in front of us, we must eat it all. We eat everything on our plate because we can't stand seeing food thrown out or wasted. Yet think of all the other things you don't hesitate to throw away. Why should food be any different?

Waste facts
Waste is waste. If you eat more than your body wants, it is waste. Whichever way you look at it, if you have eaten enough, your body doesn't need any more. The extra food is of no nutritional value, so it's waste. Look at it this way, it all gets thrown out in the end, be it in the bin or through your system into the toilet. It's better that it is thrown out through the outside system than your internal one, for waste has no place in your system; it does more harm than good. Food digesting takes up more energy than any

other bodily function. And you know this only too well — think of how lethargic and tired you feel if you have overeaten.

Yet most of us, being good little 'waste nots', won't throw food away. But leftovers can go to the family pet, be used for another meal, put into the compost bin, or be given to the neighbours or their pets. It's easy, isn't it! I want you to swear that you will now resign from the clean-plate club! Just to make sure you have the hang of it, for the next week, for at least one meal a day, I want you to leave some food on your plate after a meal, and then throw it away.

HANDY HINTS

EXPERIMENT WITH DIFFERENT LEVELS OF SATISFACTION.
AIM AT A LEVEL OF SATISFACTION THAT YOU FEEL COMFORTABLE WITH.
MAKE AN EFFORT TO LEAVE SOME FOOD ON YOUR PLATE.
IF YOU ARE NOT SURE IF YOU ARE SATISFIED ENOUGH, LEAVE THE TABLE FOR TWO MINUTES AND THEN DO A SATISFACTION LEVEL CHECK.

CHAPTER EIGHTEEN

HANDLING
SOCIAL EATING

Dieter's mind-set: Social eating is a good opportunity to eat more.

Eating out can be a frustrating time when it comes to eating what you want and stopping when you're satisfied. There is so much going on — conversations, people, abundance of food — it is difficult to really focus on stopping at a satisfaction level. Let's take a look at the most common social situations we find ourselves in.

Restaurants

I used to find restaurant eating a real problem because I was always ravenous at least two hours before I knew I would be able to eat. I would fill up on bread rolls and the entree and, by the time the main meal came around, I had little appetite left for enjoying my dinner. Yet I always found room to stuff down dessert. Most times I would overeat and go home feeling very bloated. Or, at the other extreme, I would eat a meal at home because I couldn't wait, then go out feeling not the slightest bit hungry. Yet I would eat again and not enjoy the meal at all. Sometimes I showed great self-control and hung on until the main course. That was really difficult, and if there were any hold-up of my order, I viewed it as sabotage. I couldn't get into the social scene as I was too busy watching all the food come out (mine seemed to take forever), and when my food arrived and I didn't like the dish, well, the night was ruined.

Dilemma
It's 6.00 pm and you are ready to eat — in fact you're starving — but you know it probably won't be eating time until about 8.00 pm. So what do you do?

Solution
Do some experimenting with food and satisfaction levels. I find a banana or a few biscuits and cheese satisfy me long enough, without ruining my appetite. It is important to experiment with your satisfaction levels so you can make all social events pleasurable and not painful. Ordering two entrees is often a good idea. Sharing meals with others is a lot of fun, too. And don't be ashamed to ask for a doggie bag — for you, not the dog! Remember, most people eat more than usual when they go out.

Food is to be enjoyed. You may be more than satisfied and that's okay. Just don't feel guilty, enjoy. Eating out is a real treat, which you pay for. Choose wisely and enjoy the food and the social interaction.

The smorgasbord dilemma
The word 'smorgasbord' usually conjures up permission for one gigantic pig-out for everyone. After all, they do advertise 'all you can eat'. I remember many times leaving smorgasbords so full I felt I needed to be rolled out the door. I look forward to smorgasbords now because I have the opportunity to try lots of different types of food and to be picky, leaving the foods that I don't fancy. That never used to be the case.

Solution
Only put a few food types on your plate. That way you won't get so confused with all the different taste sensations. Go for small

portions and don't over-pile your plate. Arrange food so that it is appealing to your eye. And lastly, be choosy. Get staff to take away the plates of food you don't like.

The dinner party dilemma
Eating out at other people's homes can be an extremely enjoyable experience or a real pain, depending on whether you really want to be there or not. The problem is that you cannot eat exactly what you want, and over-polite hosts who insist you eat more food than you want can get upset if you refuse. Quite often we eat politely at a dinner party, then pig out when we get home because we did not eat what we really wanted.

Solution
It's okay to leave some food on the plate. If your host takes offence, just politely explain that you are full and you want to keep room for dessert or coffee.

Talk to interesting people or about interesting topics after the meal is over (if you can!).

The 'my own dinner party dilemma'
If there ever is a time when bingeing rates a 10 on the Richter scale, it has to be at your own dinner party. There are many reasons for this: all that different food, including the food you usually forbid yourself to eat, nerves, deserving a reward for your efforts, sampling and tasting. Picture this familiar scene: It's Saturday, you are having a few work colleagues around for dinner and, as much as you hate to admit it, you are out to impress. You want approval for putting on a lovely spread — we all want some recognition for our efforts. You go and buy all your goodies on Saturday morning, lots of food you don't normally buy — yummy, delicious, tantalising foods. You spend the afternoon cleaning, cooking and preparing. You may have thrown your sensible eating out the door earlier on in the piece and decided if there was ever a good excuse for a pig-out, this is it. Or you may be adamant that you will stick to your diet, no matter what. Any

way you choose, you are still concerned with everything turning out well. I can't remember a dinner party that I actually felt hungry at and enjoyed eating my own cooking.

You sit down and eat, but don't really enjoy your meal, as you are too concerned whether everyone else is enjoying theirs. You take the plates to the kitchen, shovelling leftovers in your mouth and giving yourself generous samplings of the next course, all at the kitchen sink.

You clean a few dishes and put the leftovers into your mouth. Dessert is done. Then into the kitchen and again into the leftovers. Your guests finally leave, you fall in a heap on the couch and polish off the rest of the leftovers. You crawl into bed, having felt very little enjoyment for all your efforts. You annoyed at being so obsessed with food and at having shovelled the leftovers in.

Solutions

Before guests arrive:
- Have a snack to take the edge off your hunger.
- Keep sampling to a bare minimum.
- Make a commitment to take care of yourself and to enjoy the fruits of your labour.

When guests arrive:
- Let yourself enjoy the fruits of your labour.
- Eat sitting down and with your friends.
- Don't be in a hurry to rush off to the kitchen.
- Accept help graciously.
- When the meal is complete, sit at another table or shift the plates and clear the table.
- Keep your guests company; don't stay in the kitchen.

After your guests depart:
- If you still feel deprived, go and get a clean plate and put your food choices on it. Sit down and enjoy.
- If you clean up, put all leftovers in the fridge.
- Remind yourself that all this food will still be there in the morning.

HANDLING SOCIAL EATING

- Treat yourself: have a bath or sit and watch TV instead of getting straight into cleaning up.

Family dinner dilemma
This can be a real time bomb. When I go home to visit my parents, the first thing I do is look in the fridge. I don't know why I do this. Mum and Dad always get a good laugh because my brother does exactly the same. I suppose it's to see if things are still the same, to see those comforting foods, those familiar things that link us back to childhood.

When I used to go home, all sensible eating would go out the door and I would revert back to binge eating. There would always be plenty of food around, and having Mum say, "Eat more, darling, you can diet again when you leave" gave me all the more reason to do so. I never knew why home had such a strong hold on me. I think it's because smells and familiar surroundings took me back to being at home and I would play the role of little girl again and eat as I used to for emotional comfort.

Solutions
- Remember that you have changed, and try not to revert back to old ways.
- Take something with you from the present that relates to your personal growth: a book, pendant, or personal ornament.
- Do something just for yourself, such as taking a walk, and remind yourself of your individuality.
- Don't play victim by blaming your upbringing for your problems. You are in control.

The wonderful experience of eating alone
It is important to put aside some time to eat alone once in a while. You need to recognise, and get in touch with, your individuality and know that you are a free soul who chooses to be and live with others. Allow yourself some time to get to know yourself. It is important to do this so that you don't confuse the need to be

alone with overeating. We all need time to ourselves. Recognise that there is a need for eating alone. Once you do this you will be able to handle social eating a lot easier because you will be more aware of your needs and understand the beauty of eating together and alone. To appreciate the experience of eating alone, try eating at least one meal alone each day. Do this for one week, paying attention to how it feels having no one else to talk to. Try eating alone in a restaurant or cafe at least three times. It doesn't have to be dinner; it can be lunch. Enjoy your own company. And, most importantly, don't forget to take your time out for 15 minutes per day.

HANDY HINTS

Prepare for your hunger.

Remain aware of your eating whilst talking to others.

Take the edge off your hunger before social events.

Go for small portions.

Enjoy the food.

PART FIVE
EMOTIONAL
HAPPINESS WITHOUT FOOD

CHAPTER NINETEEN

HOW TO FEEL EMOTIONS
WITHOUT NEEDING FOOD

Eating doesn't happen on its own. Regardless of your weight, eating is always linked with some kinds of emotions and feelings. You only have to flip open magazines and see Mum there with a big smile and a plate full of scones, or a woman indulging in her favourite chocolate, or romance and intimacy on the TV with cups of coffee. Eating can be a very emotional experience. The day that we are born we associate warmth, love and safety with the breast of our mother. In childhood we get rewarded with goodies, or if we are sick, we may get our favourite food. All cultures and religions use food in a symbolic way in their customs, such as at Christmas and Easter. So many celebrations have a strong link with food. Each time we use food to soothe or comfort, our emotional bond to the food deepens. You will always eat for some emotional reasons. The key is to deal with uncomfortable feelings without turning to food. This is what we will be exploring now. Once you can master this, your life will be given an unbelievable boost, and losing weight will seem just an added bonus.

If we eat at the first trigger of an uncomfortable feeling, we start linking the food with special qualities such as love, comfort, rewards, happiness and friendship. It can be quite embarrassing to admit our neediness with food, but it is not as difficult as telling people we love of our neediness. Many of us become quite surprised by this issue because we have buried emotions for so long with food that we don't even realise what we are doing. This is because we never let the feelings surface and, at the first hint of discomfort, we turn to food. When we eat instead of feeling an emotion, we push that emotion down even further, and most of us are not even sure what feelings we are experiencing, blaming our weight for feeling miserable.

Not knowing how to handle difficult emotions or anxiety, we eat. Some people drink, some people smoke and some of us eat. How many times have you reached for food not really knowing why, not really hungry, but feeling a touch anxious? Before you even had time to think what was making you anxious, you finished eating a packet of chips, biscuits or whatever you could lay your hands on. This is emotional eating. We reach for food when we experience anxiety making us feel uncomfortable. We suppress the rising emotion with food rather than express it.

What then happens is we start blaming all uncomfortable feelings on our weight. It is far easier to deal with the weight issue than all the other issues we have hidden underneath our weight. Then we say, "Oh, but if I were slim, I wouldn't have any of these problems". If you believe this, just ask the next slim person you meet if he or she is happy! We would not focus so much on our body if we felt more comfortable expressing our thoughts and feelings more openly.

The key is to first understand what is happening and then equip yourself with the tools to help you experience and deal with your uncomfortable feelings. Let's get this straight at once: no feeling is negative. All feelings you have, even the painful ones, are there to help you. We are told it is not right to express anger or frustration, but the longer you deny feeling an emotion, the worst it gets; until one day you may explode over what is seemingly nothing and others around will ask what is wrong with you. They will say that you are so emotional, letting a little thing like that upset you so much. This is where many of us get the label of being over-emotional and irrational, when all that bottled-up emotion one day just explodes.

Another important point is that no emotion you have is too difficult to deal with. Life will never dish out what you can't handle.

The stages of emotional eating
Most dieters will eat for emotional reasons most of the time. Food can help out in so many ways, from alleviating mild boredom and restlessness through to soothing extremely difficult emotions, such as 'uncontrollable' anger. Eating in this way is not triggered by physical hunger. It is important to realise that emotional eating develops in stages of intensity, from mild to severe sedation. Let us take a closer look at the stages; they are very helpful in understanding what situations trigger your eating. This information is fundamental for changing the way you use food.

1. Using food as a treat
The mildest and most common use of food is for pleasure. If you deprive yourself emotionally you will get your pleasure from another source. In our case, this is usually food. From a reward for working hard to a reward for finishing a job, we can and do invent so many ways to treat ourselves with food. Many people without weight problems use food as a treat as well. The difference is they really enjoy the treat without any feelings of guilt and afterwards just get along with the next thing in their day. Also, most 'treat eating' is spontaneous; it doesn't become habitual.

2. Using food for comfort
Whenever I get sick I always feed myself tomato soup and soldier toasts. It is a sign of comfort for me as my mother used to do that for me when I was a child. Do you do the same? Connections between food and comfort go very deep. There is no need to stop

this; it is a normal part of your eating cycle. Everyone does it. Nothing beats drinking a hot cocoa curled up by the fire. Enjoy these moments, as they are special. It gets out of hand when you turn to food for comfort *most of the time* just because you don't know any other way to get comfort. Food is the only thing that comes to mind to take care of you if you are sad or lonely.

3. Using food to distract
If we explore a little further the stages of emotional eating, we will arrive at distraction. This is where food starts to become an issue — we leave comforters and treats behind. We use food as a distraction when we want to cover up feelings we don't wish to experience or don't know how to deal with. Distraction eating is my weakness.

This section on emotional eating has been the most difficult part of the book for me to write. Every time I started on this section I would get up, go to the kitchen and eat. As a result, many foods have been consumed in writing this section, but now that I have finetuned my awareness, I can work out what is going on — unlike in the past, when I would just keep eating until I felt the urge to stop. As I start to eat I tune into my feelings and I notice that I always feel anger and frustration in this part of the book, probably because it is on emotions and this can be quite a complex issue. Then I go outside and do some deep breathing and go for a short walk around the garden. By this stage I am fully composed again and I can start to look at what is really going on.

For me the frustration covers the deeper issues in myself that I still have to deal with. Looking deeper, I find when I start to feel insecure about myself, I get frustrated and still turn to food with feelings of being 'a bit hopeless'. But I now have embedded deeply, through years of training, some very important thought patterns which are conducive to my growth and stop me from falling into the seduction of a distraction-eating pattern. These thought patterns are:

HOW TO FEEL EMOTIONS WITHOUT NEEDING FOOD

(i) There will always be times when I will turn to food, such as when I am having a difficult time dealing with an emotion.
(ii) As soon as I am aware I am doing this, I can stop.
(iii) I forgive myself for not being perfect and I love and accept myself just the way I am.

Throughout my dieting years, before I learnt awareness, I would eat at the slightest feeling of frustration and keep on eating in an oblivious state. I wouldn't ever try to find out what was troubling me. This is the way that so many of us live. If we continue to eat in this state we start to think of food as more than just food; we start using it as a painkiller, soother and comforter. This brings us to the next stage of how we use food.

4. Using food as a painkiller/soother

In my dieting days I would frequently lapse into this stage, and life would become one long binge. I would lock myself away, call in sick from work and stay in bed all day. When we get to this stage, it indicates that something is seriously wrong. However, most of us wouldn't have a clue what it is because we are too alienated from the original source, which has been buried very deep down below. Let's face reality: no matter how much pain we are in, food cannot get rid of feelings, food cannot make things better, food can never fill that emotional hole that you are trying to fill. Food only numbs us and we feel worse after we have eaten — but now with *two* issues to deal with, overeating and excess weight. At the end of the day we are still faced with the situations that turned us to food in the first place. We suffer then because, instead of experiencing and working through situations, we stop, eat, and hide our emotions and they just get pushed down deeper and deeper. And this can lead us to the final stage on the emotional eating cycle.

5. Using food as punishment

The longer we stay with the numbing effect of using food as a painkiller, the more likely we will move into this stage, which is very similar to a binge episode. Sometimes we find ourselves so angry that we eat in a forceful manner, pushing the food down as a type of self-punishment. This leads to loss of self-esteem and hatred of one's self. Underneath it all, we feel extremely hurt and vulnerable.

You will probably see your own pattern in these five stages. Most of us will be in one, two, if not all, stages every day of our lives. This understanding will now help you put practices in place to reduce the amount and severity of your emotional eating. So let's move on.

Foods and their emotional link

In my experience I have observed that there are certain foods we tend to gravitate towards in different emotional states. My anger and frustration days involve hard chewy foods, like nutty bars, to really get my teeth and jaw grinding. When I eat them I know straight away what's happening. This chart will help make you aware of what foods you go running to and why you go running to them.

FEELING	NEED	FOOD	REASON
Anger	Release	Hard chewy foods	Involve the teeth
Lonely	Nurturing	Warm foods: soups Smooth foods: milk and ice-cream	Feel and give warmth
Deprived	Pleasure	Sweets or treat foods	Give pleasure
Bored	Excitement	Spicy, strong flavours	Give rush
Tired	Energy	Carbohydrates, sugar	Raise blood sugar
Sexual	Sensuality	Sweets, chocolate	Satisfy senses
Unloved	Hugs and kisses	Sweets, treats	Feel special

Remember, as I said before, emotional eating is part of life, but the key is to make it a balanced part, not the whole of your life. Next time you run to food as an emotional fix, talk to the food, aloud if you can, and ask what it is that you want it to do for you. How do you want to feel? Write all this down. Allow yourself to feel whatever emotion it is. In order to stop emotional eating, this confrontation with ourselves first is critical. We must start to realise that food is not magical; it can't do everything for us. Feeling awful and uncomfortable is part of the road to recovery. Feelings are there to be experienced. You don't have to get rid of them; just recognise and accept them.

HANDY HINTS

Explore your relationship with food.
Find a link to your emotional state and highest food intake.
Try to start separating the two.

CHAPTER TWENTY

ACTIVATE YOUR POWER
FOR EMOTIONAL MASTERY

Whenever you find yourself eating a lot from emotional hunger, it's time to go within yourself and see what is going on. The core situations that will turn most of us to food are:
1. Feeling in danger or overwhelmed by your feelings.
2. Feeling guilty for your thoughts or feelings.
3. Feeling that you are a failure.

Do you experience these types of thoughts daily? To help this situation you must first make sure you are following the eating success steps:

1. Are you always allowing yourself to eat when you are physically hungry?

Eating when you are physically hungry is the fundamental cure for emotional hunger. Think about it: if you deny yourself the basic need of eating when your hunger asks to be fed, it begins to feel deprived and this deprivation gets translated into, and mixed with other painful emotions. We then turn to food to comfort us and to help us cope.

2. Have you really legalised all food?

Because if you haven't, these foods still have power over you, and you are still thinking about and using them in magical ways.

3. Have you an abundance of all your favourite foods around you?

If you don't, you will begin to feel deprived on an emotional and physical level. Are you regularly doing activities that comfort and nurture you? Depriving yourself of the simple pleasures in life will send you running to food.

Steps to help you on the inside

1. The only way to deal with painful emotions is to experience them here and now

They are not bad, they are your teachers. Once you understand this you really accelerate your personal growth. Living in the present means being honest enough to avoid the easy emotions of anger and frustration and to expose the hurt, which is harder to confront. When the hurt is not resolved in the present, the vicious build-up of anger, guilt and depression can only grow worse. Feeling a painful emotion and understanding where it came from is often not enough to make you feel better. Be with your sensations and resist the impulse either to deny what you feel or to turn it into anger. Being in the moment, by putting your attention on the hurt, allows you to release the hurt as soon as it occurs. But you need to go one step further: you need to nurture yourself on the inside. This is done by kind self-talk and kind actions to yourself.

2. Express how you feel

Talk to the person who caused the hurt. Draw or write down your feelings. Start getting them out.

3. Deep breathe!

I cannot emphasise enough the benefits that deep breathing will bring you, physically and emotionally. Breathing releases emotions. When you hold emotions in, you hold your breath and push them down further. Release your breath deeply and you will begin to release anxiety, worry, fear and uncomfortable emotions. Do this as soon as you begin to feel something. If you do it two hours later, you will have already stored the emotion. Again, awareness is the key. All painful emotions experienced are to be learnt from. Examine them and, when you are finished, put them in an imaginary bubble and send them on their merry way to the land of oblivion.

4. Look at your belief system and reassess your pain

Is your belief causing you unnecessary pain? Try to see it objectively. Choose an emotion that you feel uncomfortable with and which you are not able to get rid of. Think back to how many times, over the past few weeks, you have experienced this emotion. Is there a situation or person that triggers it off? Re-enact the scene with your eyes closed. How do you feel about yourself when you experience this emotion? What do you want to do there and then? How long after experiencing this feeling do you turn to food? What type of food do you turn to? Now visualise telling the people or person involved how you feel. What emotions come up for you? Breathe deeply when doing this exercise and at any time you feel anxious about a situation or emotion.

We have discussed earlier how our beliefs affect what we eat and how we view food and our body. Let us now look into the set of beliefs you have that affects you emotionally and causes you much unnecessary suffering. As an example, let's consider a simple scenario on politeness. Do you get annoyed with people who do not acknowledge you in the mornings? You know the type — they just come in, sit down and start work. They never bother to say 'good morning', and are always rude and abrupt. We believe in manners, don't we? We have been brought up to be polite and we disapprove of rudeness, so we let these people, the 'rudies' of the world, annoy us.

Sometimes you might get on your high horse and give them a lecture on politeness. They either stare blankly or tell you, not so politely, where to go. Now think about it, why should people say good morning all the time, just because you think they should? Does politeness make you a better person? The more rules and regulations you impose on yourself and others, the more miserable you become as you try desperately to mould people to fit into your world. We need to relax some of our thought patterns and challenge our beliefs so that we do not get bogged down in negative emotions all the time. Your beliefs make you think a certain way, and then follow the emotions which make you react in that same way.

The following situation highlights again the way our belief system rules how we feel and act emotionally.

Situation: Party scene one
You are at a party and there are many slim, attractive women there. You start to feel very uncomfortable and start judging yourself and others. You sit in the corner, eating, and giving each person that walks past the third degree in your mind. A slim and attractive woman comes over to you and tries to make conversation. You find it very painful as you are blinded by judgments and jealousy. You just want to go home, for you believe being fat makes you miserable. You make an excuse to get away.

Belief:
Slim, attractive people are better than me. Being fat means I can't have fun. I am unworthy of having fun.

Emotion:
Depression, resentment, guilt.

Action:
Not very talkative at party; leave early. What you have to do is go deeper than the 'fat feeling'. It is just the surface.

Being able to increase your awareness of your beliefs and how they affect your emotions and actions will help you become more aware of why you eat when you are not hungry. The aim is to learn to satisfy emotional hungers without food. It is okay to have good and bad feelings. It is not a crime to feel sad. Allow yourself to experience the feelings. Do not rush to food. We are not taught to deal with negative emotions very well in our society. Therefore we do not let them surface — we squash them and block them out with food. It takes time, gentleness and compassion for ourselves, but the rewards are truly great — happiness.

Write down which emotions you have a problem with and why.

Emotions start to cause us problems when the beliefs behind them are irrational. Start disputing and facing these irrational beliefs. Challenge them and change them.

Now let's recreate the same scenario as in scene one, but we'll change our belief and reaction.

Party scene: Take two
Emotion:
Feeling depressed. Why?
Belief:
Thin people are better than me.
Challenge belief:
Why do I believe this? People are all the same. I am just as good as the next. I love and respect myself.
Feeling:
Not so bad, keep affirming my new belief.
Action:
Talk more at party, start to enjoy myself.

The only way to change these deeply embedded, harmful beliefs is by picking up on them as soon as they arise and inserting new positive beliefs. Some beliefs are so deeply embedded we believe them to be true. A very common one for many of us is 'I am no good'. Working with an experienced counsellor is a very good idea if you are overwhelmed with negative beliefs about yourself.

5. Break the pattern of criticism

Self-criticism is one of the biggest issues that we have to deal with when we are overweight. Remaining overweight protects us from the criticism we get from others and ourselves. Some of us are so cruel to ourselves with criticism that even when people say something complimentary to us we immediately think negatively: "They only say that because they pity me". We tend to criticise the same thing about ourselves over and over again. Statements like "I am too fat", "I am useless" and "I have no willpower" seem to dominate our thought patterns. These types of thoughts will only keep you in victim mode and will drag you further down the spiral of self-hate and self-pity.

Self-criticism is a difficult pattern to break, for you have probably been subjected to it from an early age. You have picked it up somewhere along the line, maybe from your parents, teachers or peer group. But if you want to break the habit, don't blame them. Start to take responsibility now.

Our Inner Critic is so deeply ingrained. It is such a familiar voice in us that we think it *is* us. Every time you catch yourself thinking that you are the Inner Critic, stop and repeat an affirmation of self-love such as, "I love you just the way you are".

Self-criticism is lack of self-love. It is a tough one to crack but the main keys are: have awareness when you are in self-criticism and replace these thoughts *immediately* with positive affirmations. And keep going. It will take many months or years to get to self-love. Remember how long you have been self-criticising, so give yourself ample time to change.

A friend of mine suggested that I wear a rubber band on my hand and flick myself every time I have a negative thought changing it to a positive one. My wrist was very red for quite some time, so I changed to hat elastic! But it worked well, because awareness is half the battle, and the band was awareness. You must become aware! It is so easy to go a whole day and forget to undo harmful self-talk because most of the time we operate in a robot-like, conditioned mode. Thus anything out of the ordinary that you can do to remind yourself and wake your senses up is great.

So there we have the secrets for feeling confident enough to let ourselves experience any kind of unpleasant thoughts and emotions. The power comes from understanding and knowing what is happening and being equipped to help yourself. After all, you are your best teacher.

ACTIVATE YOUR POWER FOR EMOTIONAL MASTERY

HANDY HINTS

Create an effective way to catch your negative thoughts when they arise.

Repeat your positive affirmations while you do your daily routines.

Find ways to keep your sense of humour.

CHAPTER TWENTY-ONE

PERSONAL POWER COMES FROM EXPLORING EMOTIONS

In a leading USA journal on weight loss, a survey conducted over 12 months by a group of psychologists working with a number of overweight women revealed that the most difficult emotions all these women had to deal with were guilt, anger, frustration, boredom, sadness and depression. This seems to be the case in all my workshops as well. So let's take a look at these and other emotions.

Guilt
Guilt rates pretty high on the list of commonly felt emotions. The reasons we feel guilty are plentiful: we feel guilty for eating too much, for eating the wrong foods, for not paying enough attention to our partner, for neglecting to spend time with our children, for indulging in something that we enjoy, for not cooking a meal.

We, as women, have the traditional role of nurturer. Whether we like it or not, we are involved in choosing, buying and cooking food for our family. We are surrounded by food and have the responsibility of feeding our family and keeping them healthy. If something goes wrong, we immediately take the blame and others are quick to judge our skills. In my experience, working mothers carry a huge amount of guilt and have a delicate balancing act to maintain of caring for themselves and their family. How do we comfort ourselves when we feel guilty? Again with food.

Exercise:
Answer the following questions to help understand your guilt: I feel guilty about ... Why do I feel guilt about ...? Is this a rational or irrational feeling?

Too much guilt indicates low self-esteem, so work on self-esteem and your guilt feelings will diminish.

Releasing anger/frustration

I have found that overweight women have more difficulty expressing anger than any other emotion. Many overweight, seemingly happy, jolly people are very unhappy inside. If we do not express how we feel, the anger builds up inside and we tend to get angry and frustration usually about the same thing over and over again. As women, most of us have never learnt how to express anger, or even to acknowledge it as an appropriate feeling, and so we have learnt to suppress it in the subconscious mind. It remains there for life or until we process it out of ourselves. As mentioned earlier, the very first emotions that surface when we cannot express our feelings are anger and frustration. Underneath these feelings lies the true source of our pain, buried so deep that when it surfaces we may not know what to do or say. As I have said before: You will never experience an emotion that you can't handle — life doesn't work like that.

Repressing anger leads to depression, guilt, bitterness, resentment and illness. If you don't release the anger you will, more than likely, turn to food. Food will kill some of the angry energy you feel and it will, just for the moment, make you too full to move or to feel and will fill the void left by your unfinished anger. But not for long. Soon you will have to deal

PERSONAL POWER COMES FROM EXPLORING EMOTIONS

with your emotions again as they will keep coming up until you deal with them. Until you deal directly with your anger you will feel unsatisfied. This dissatisfaction will lead to a large hunger that you will keep wanting to fill with food, and it will not disappear until you learn to express your anger.

When we have so much bottled-up anger and blocked emotions inside, it is because we are unable to express how we feel. To understand why we feel like this we must look back into our past conditioning about anger and about expressing emotions.

What did you do with the anger you felt as a child?

Did you feel it was safe to express anger?

How did your parents show anger?

Do your repress your anger?

Are you feeling angry at the same things that made you angry as a child?

What pattern of anger is your style: shouting, screaming, the silent treatment, rudeness?

To express anger as a child, did you throw a tantrum, run away, cry or sulk, hit someone, rebel, act rudely? What do you do now when you express anger? Do you yell and scream, cry, confront, become sarcastic, overeat?

What happened when you expressed your anger as a child? Were you ignored, punished, listened to, rejected? Does this still happen to you now?

I used to have great difficulty telling someone that she or he had upset me. This, in turn, led me to become angry and frustrated. I am not good with quick comebacks or smart comments and I used to just seethe and stew over people and situations, conjuring up in my mind what I should have said or done. I used to grit my teeth when family or friends told me what I should or should not eat. I would either snap back at them or silently seethe.

The solution is to just say how you feel. You don't have to be a smart; just let the other person know how you feel. It is far easier than trying to have a comeback line. A comment like, 'I get angry when you tell me what I should eat' is enough. You do not have to go on and on. Just say how you feel and more words will come later if you need to express yourself more. One woman I know is still silently seething two years after a doctor told her all her health problems were due to her being too fat. Still, to this very day, she conjures up what she should have told the doctor. It is better just to get it out, even if it is on paper or via a phone call.

Remember:
- You have the right to get angry. Allow yourself to get angry.
- Yell and scream and let it out of your system.
- You can tell someone you are angry without being hurtful.
- You can get angry and still be loved.
- To release long-stored anger you can:
  - Write a letter to that particular person and then post or burn the letter.
  - Talk directly to the person involved. Say, 'I am angry at you because ...'
  - Recognise anger, try to identify what made you angry and let it out.
  - Scream in the car with all the windows up. Bash your fists into your pillow.
  - Visualise the scene with the person who made you angry and let out your anger. In the scene talk to this person, saying how you feel.

Exercise:
Answer the following questions to help explore your anger:
- Anger is often a fear — what are you afraid of losing?
- What situations make you instantly angry?
- What makes you feel that things won't happen unless you get angry? For example, telling the children to clean their room.
- Ask yourself: Why do I always get angry when ...? How does it help me ...? What other way can I react ...?

The key with anger is to recognise, accept, keep breathing deeply, check your beliefs and see the big picture. Just getting angry all the time will not help bring up unsolved emotional issues. I suggest reading *The Dance of Anger* by Harriet Letber, a great book for exploring and dealing with anger in practical and useful ways.

Boredom

Boredom is a very common reason women give for turning to food. But just what is being bored all about? Boredom is not really an emotion; it is a state of mind. People say, "I'm happy", "I'm sad", "I'm bored". Boredom usually comes from not being able to identify a blocked feeling or emotion and not knowing what to do with it. In my experience I have found that boredom and depression go hand-in-hand. I have never seen a happy bored person. The usual pattern with being bored is one of a 'couldn't-be-bothered' attitude and a nagging feeling of restlessness and depression which you can't quite put your finger on. Your personality does not like being bored because by being bored you are getting closer to your blocked emotions. Boredom drives us to fill our time with trivia because it is the state we enter into just before we find out something about ourselves that we have been burying for many years, something which may not be so pleasant. Boredom is the state we enter into that creates a layer over the blocked emotion. By learning to explore and express your feelings, that frustrated feeling you get when you are bored will slowly disappear. The most important thing when you are feeling bored is to deep breathe, try to get past the bored feeling and discover what emotions are lying underneath.

Sadness/depression

It is quite common for us to turn to food when we are sad. Depression stems from not following our true feelings and in holding down anger. Depression is inward anger, when you feel you 'shouldn't have'. For example, you might get angry at your children, then you feel guilty for being angry at your children, then you get depressed. Once you reach the depressed stage, it is pretty hard to get out of the 'poor me' syndrome which leads to self-talk such as, "I'm so depressed that getting out of bed is a real effort". This 'poor me' talk sends you very quickly down the spiral of despair. So it is important to get your feelings and thoughts out on paper or to a person.

Fear/anxiety

Overeating is a way of not feeling fear. Fear is not having trust in yourself and not accepting your own unique, wonderful gifts and talents. Remember the old saying, 'Ninety-eight per cent of what you fear won't happen'? Fear comes from inside of us, from our belief system, and most of it is totally irrational. Whose fears are you holding onto? Are they rational? Get these beliefs out on paper and start disputing them. Again, breathe through your fear; don't let it strangle you. A great book to read is *Feel the Fear and Do it Anyway* by Susan Jefferies.

Resentment

Anger that has been buried for a long time turns to resentment, which lodges itself deep in our bodies. If not expressed, it causes us physical illness. Deeply suppressed emotions take a little bit of cajoling to bring to the surface. Often it is easier to get sick and to hold onto the bitterness and resentment. Resentment is a fear of losing out: "If I forgive them, I will feel vulnerable and they will have one over me." Forgiving can be a very challenging but rewarding action to take. Ask yourself: Who is the winner, a body full of resentment, which is not healthy, or a body that is prepared to release and forgive and, in the process, become healthier?

HANDY HINTS

ALWAYS BREATHE DEEPLY WHEN YOU ARE EXPERIENCING UNPLEASANT EMOTIONS.
RELEASE THE EMOTION IN THE MOMENT THAT IT ARISES.
NO EMOTION CAN CONTROL YOU UNLESS YOU LET IT.
IF AN EMOTION ARISES WITHOUT AN OUTSIDE INFLUENCE CAUSING IT TO ARISE, IT IS JUST COMING UP TO BE RELEASED.
IT IS MERELY A CLEARING OF OLD 'STUFF' WHICH IS BETTER OUT OF YOUR SYSTEM.

PERSONAL POWER COMES FROM EXPLORING EMOTIONS

Don't fall into the trap of playing out old emotions again and again. Just let them go, and move on.

Don't get depressed feeling these emotions, for they are a part of life. Knowing what they are and recognising them gives you the power to express and explore them. Don't fear them; they are great teachers in life.

PART SIX

HOW TO LIKE
YOUR BEAUTIFUL BODY

CHAPTER TWENTY-TWO

THIGHS, LIES AND
BODY IMAGE

How many times have you fantasised about becoming so thin that you would be the envy of all women and the lust of all men? The media and our society fuel this fantasy and tell us that thin women are attractive, thin women always get the men they want, thin women never have problems — basically that being thin is the greatest state. We spend our whole life wishing to be thin and, in the process, we live our life away in fantasy land. We tend to view our bodies as either fat or thin, nothing else. There is so much more to you than external appearance. Our society is totally infatuated and obsessed with external beauty. Just listen to the language we speak. The 'when I get thin' language is almost our mother tongue. Next time you are with a group of friends, try not to make any comment on your body or anybody else's or food intake — and see the conversation halt.

Our body image and food intake go hand-in-hand. When we eat more than we think we should, we tend to feel negative about our body size. We then become judgmental about what we are eating and bring in our negative thoughts, which reflect dissatisfaction with our body size. A typical scenario is the ritual of looking at ourselves in the mirror, hating what we see and then heading for the kitchen. Years of dieting have made us believe that our body is only to be liked when we eat less and weigh less. Thus we begin to truly believe that 'life isn't worth enjoying when I'm fat'.

Dieter's belief: Only when I lose weight will I like my body and enjoy myself.

It is such a shame that we are always waiting until we get thin to enjoy our life. Think of all the good times you have let pass by because you thought you were too fat to enjoy them, or you were so engrossed in the misery of your weight that nothing could possibly have been enjoyable. Comments such as, "If my legs get thinner, then I will be happier" or, "As soon as I flatten my tummy, I will go to the beach" keep us stuck in victim mode and never allow us to be truly happy.

The beach used to be my favourite cop-out. I never used to enjoy myself because I was too busy comparing my figure with other women's, and a swim was only on the cards if there was no one around. And I would only get out of the water when the coast was clear. Then it would be a mad dash up to the towel. Parties were another sad episode. If I did decide to go to a party, I would spend hours choosing or buying an outfit that would make me look the least fat. I would spend my time judging other women's bodies, getting stuck into the food and have a few drinks to drown my anguish and self-pity, hating my body so much for making me so miserable. I'm sure you have many similar sad tales to tell.

The word 'fat' has only recently been slurred. The Latin word for 'fat' means 'fertile' or 'copious'. English definitions include: well filled out, fleshy, plump, fertile. I'm sure you have seen all those wonderful paintings of larger women in art galleries, and I bet your thoughts were, "Wouldn't it be good if larger women were seen as beautiful again? All my problems would be over". The reality is that we live in a society infatuated with thinness. However, we don't have to be part of the scene. We can opt out of the body infatuation stakes. Now I'm not saying, "stay fat and be happy", but what I am trying to get you to see is the broader picture (no pun intended), and how narrow our thinking is when it comes to acceptable body sizes.

Really start to challenge the source of all your negative thoughts. What are your negative body thoughts? Where did these thoughts come from? Family, the media, our culture? You did not start out life with negative thoughts about your body. They take time to develop and are fed by what you have been told in the past, by the people you surround yourself with now and by what you see and hear in your environment. Rarely are we taught from our mothers or other women how wonderful our bodies are, regardless of our body shape. From the time we are very young, we see our mothers or other females criticising their bodies. So we grow up alienated from our body. The other day I heard a woman say, "I just pretend my body doesn't exist". It is very sad to get to that stage — how can you pretend a part of you is not there?

Our culture is a reflection of how we think about thin and fat people. What are your thoughts on thin women? Are they something like this: Thin women are sexually attractive, happy, young, admired. What about your thoughts about fat people? Miserable, unattractive, messy, unhappy. Carefully examine your own thoughts on fat and thin women, for they are what you really think about yourself!

A friend of mine met me in the shopping mall the other day. As she approached me I thought, *Wow, she looks great*! She was smiling from ear to ear, walking with grace, wearing a beautiful outfit which looked extremely feminine and really made her features stand out. I told her she looked fabulous. She looked at me, horrified, and then pulled up her jacket, stuck out her stomach and said: "Fabulous? look at this!" She started to poke her stomach, calling it 'horrible, jellyfish flab'. I asked her what she thought of the rest of her body. Her reply was: "I don't think about it much. I'm too obsessed with this gut of mine." She believed that to the outside world she looked grossly obese, when in reality she looked great! It's sad, isn't it? That is what negative body thoughts do to you.

Your inner self loves you the way you are. Unfortunately, you have conditioned yourself with the judgments from external sources. My change from self-hate to self-love took me quite a few years. I started with self-acceptance. I realised that I had this wonderful body that I had treated so harshly with self-abuse. So I decided to start accepting what I had. I began to neutralise the negative thoughts I had about my body. Instead of thinking, "I hate my big fat thighs", I started saying, "My legs are strong and healthy; they take me everywhere I want to go". Gradually, over time, self-acceptance grew into self-love and, as a side effect from treating myself with kindness and looking after my well-being, I started to lose weight.

The body obsession stakes

The other day on the beach I overheard two (slim) women talking to each other. Their conversation went like this:

Woman 1: "I told Faye she should lose some weight. All those fatty foods she eats — no wonder she is so fat".

Woman 2: "I know, it's awful! But look at me. I'm turning into a beach ball. Look at this (pinch of half a millimetre of fat round the midriff) — it's so gross. I feel so ugly."

Woman 1: (Sees larger lady walking along beach) "Hey, look at that. How can she let herself get like that? Look at her — she thinks she can wear a bikini looking like that! That is gross. They should have beach police to tell her to get off."

Woman 1: "Oh, you know Jan? The one who lost 15 kilogrammes? Have you noticed all the guys checking her out? She thinks she is *too* good now. Hey, what do you want for lunch?"

Woman 2: "I'm not eating. I was so naughty and ate

half a Mars bar at 10.00 am. I'm going to starve till dinner, then have a salad."

What a wonderfully enlightening conversation, just bursting with intelligence and self-love! But how often do you hear, or are a part of, this type of talk? Diet and slimness obsession is embedded in our culture as a language all its own. Appreciating physical beauty is fine, but not when it becomes obsessive and reduces your self-image to zero. Admire, accept, and get along with your life. Why hang onto the pain of the image of beauty and slenderness? It just prevents you from enjoying your own uniqueness. If you truly want to take care of yourself and lose some weight, you must start accepting and liking yourself NOW. Otherwise, regardless of your shape, you will always find fault. The change must start today and grow steadily and slowly. One, small change in your thinking will lead to dramatic change in your life.

Stop this poking, jabbing, grabbing and hitting parts of your body, pulling and pinching it as if it were some foreign devil! How can we ever make peace with ourselves if we handle our bodies in such a degrading way?

Every time you say you feel fat, you are saying, "There is something wrong with me". What you are really feeling is self-hate and self-disgust. Turning your focus onto your body keeps your true thoughts and feelings under control. "I feel fat" translates into "safer to be fat and hide the way I really feel". You know that the problem you attempt to solve with dieting is not a 'fat problem' but is, instead, the way you feel about yourself as a woman. Therefore, no matter how thin you get, you will still feel fat, larger than what you consider appropriate, unless you change now. When negative body thoughts overwhelm you and rule your life, you then resort to desperate measures like stapling, liposuction and other drastic treatments. This temporary distraction keeps you focused on the fat and not on the underlying issues.

Yesterday on television I watched a program about a lady who had just had liposuction. She was paraded around like some prize pony as the doctor poked and prodded where the fat had been taken out, commenting on how beautiful she looked now. The lady said that her husband thought she looked fantastic. I'll bet my bottom dollar that after the novelty and the emotions that go with the new look wear off, all her painful emotions will rise to the surface again. This woman will then do something else externally to make her feel loved again. External measures are not the answer. True healing for positive change and everlasting happiness must come from within.

So we know now that a negative body thought is never really about your body. But this is sometimes hard to understand. After all, when we get a 'fat attack', all we think of is how gross, ugly and revolting our bodies are. Although looking in the mirror is what makes you feel awful about your thighs, hips, buttocks or stomach, something else is happening inside you which you conceal by focusing on your body. This focus disguises the real problems. When you are having negative body thoughts, you are attacking your body instead of allowing yourself to think or feel something else. You then lose track of what you are feeling and become convinced that fat is your problem. The benefits of, course, are simplicity: one problem — fat; one solution — diet.

Most of us have become so accustomed to negative body thoughts that we find it hard to convince ourselves that we have real issues or concerns underneath it all. Negative body thoughts are hard to let go of because they are such an effective way to conceal other anxieties. In a whirlwind of confused thoughts, mixed in with some 'illegal' foods and 'illegal' quantities, what you do is focus totally on feelings about food and fat. As painful as it is to abuse ourselves constantly with bad thoughts, they are at least straightforward and less complex than the issues they mask. But as long as we continue to focus our energy on negative body thoughts, our pain will continue and things will not change.

HANDY HINTS

Start accepting your body for what it does rather than what it looks like.

Challenge negative thoughts about your body and neutralise them.

CHAPTER TWENTY-THREE
HOW TO LIKE THE
WHOLE PACKAGE

We all come in different shapes and sizes, yet the media seems quite oblivious to this, portraying women as skinny, thin, skeletal. The reality is that each one of us is so uniquely different. It is ironic that 95 per cent of us are not magazine-straight-up-and-down thin, which is what the media prey on. It keeps the money coming in. They know the extraordinary lengths and costs we will go to look like the body beautiful, so we will be liked. But I don't have to tell you that this is a path of never-ending sadness and self-hate. The real change, however, must first come from within. Negative thoughts about our bodies occupy the minds of the majority of women.

Exercise:
How does a negative body thought affect you? Picture in your mind your daily routine, what you did over the past 24 hours. Write down each activity and then next to each activity, write down the type of thought you had about your body.

Part 1

ACTIVITY	NEGATIVE THOUGHT
Getting out of bed	Here we go again, another day in this fat ugly body.
Taking a shower	I hate being fat. I wish I could just cut it off.
Getting dressed	What can I wear that makes me look half decent?

Part 2 — your body parts

Write down the following body parts: Face, neck, shoulders, breasts, arms, hands, stomach, buttocks, thighs, calves, feet. Then write down your thoughts and feelings about them. Then write a neutralising statement about the negative statements you wrote.

For example:

Body part	Thoughts	Neutralising statement
Thighs	Fat, wobbly, gross	My legs are strong and carry me around

This exercise certainly makes you aware of how many negative thoughts you have about your body. It may seem quite a struggle writing a neutralising statement about some of your body parts, those that you feel really disgusted about, but persist. It is very important to finish. Don't let your Inner Critic walk all over you. Show it that you really do accept yourself on a deep level.

There is a great saying, 'What you focus on you get'. If your focus is on how much you hate your body, is it any wonder that you do? Most of us separate our bodies into segments which we feel disgusted about, such as 'fat stomach', 'big bum', 'flabby arms', and we never see the real picture of our total package. When you meet someone, you don't automatically look at their body parts, do you? No, you see them as a whole package. It is only because we have become completely paranoid about our body parts not being up to standard that we have a completely distorted view of our bodies. An exercise I get women to do in my workshop is to draw themselves. In 90 per cent of cases, they draw grossly exaggerated images of huge body parts.

HOW TO LIKE THE WHOLE PACKAGE

Along with eliminating negative body thoughts, you need to come back and live in your body, not pretend it doesn't exist. Treat yourself with love and compassion. Take small steps. Going from self-hate to self-love is a long process. Start to work on self-acceptance first. I find that body movement exercises such as Tai Chi and Yoga are a great way to learn more about your body and give you a deeper understanding of its workings and how it links to the mind and soul.

Start viewing your body as a whole, not as chunks of meat you don't like. You have to live with your body 24 hours a day — this is quite a battle if you hate yourself. How can I love something I hate so much, you might ask? We all have a unique shape. When you accept the idea that you are willing to like yourself just the way you are, you are not playing the 'body image game', and you give the power back to yourself.

The body is a wonderful machine and takes us though the journey of life. It is up to you whether this journey is pleasurable or painful. You need to take care of your body regardless of your weight. By experiencing and understanding your body for what it really is you will not feel you have lost your protective 'fat coat' when you do start to lose weight.

HANDY HINTS

THINK UP A FEW NEUTRALISING STATEMENTS FOR THE BODY PARTS YOU DISLIKE THE MOST.
RE-AFFIRM THESE STATEMENTS FREQUENTLY.
DO SOME BODY MOVEMENT THAT IS GENTLE AND KIND TO YOUR BODY.

CHAPTER TWENTY-FOUR

CLOTHES SIZE
VICTIMS

Dieter's belief: Wearing nice clothes is only for slim people.

How many wardrobes do you have? I'll bet my bottom dollar there is a thin, fat and in-between section in your wardrobe. The clothes we wear tell us so much about ourselves: the way we feel, the things we do. Let's look at this more closely. Picture this scene: You wake up feeling fat from a binge the night before and you go to your wardrobe and pick out your 'fat outfit' to wear. What does it look like? Loose, and dark in colour? What does it do for your figure? What does it do for your emotions? Do you hide in it? Is it safe?

So on goes the 'fat dress', and you instantly take on the role of a 'fat person'. You woke up feeling fat and you took action to be that way by wearing your fat dress. And you will probably finish the role by eating 'fat' too.

We give our clothes tremendous power over us. If you were to get dressed in a happy mood, what would you wear today? What about if you were feeling fat? Powerful? How different would your dress be? We play out many roles with words, actions and clothes. When I ask women in my workshops what their fat wardrobe looks like, without a doubt the clothes are all dark, drab, dreary and unflattering. 'Why do you wear them then?' I ask. The excuses are: "You can't get nice clothes from a size 14 up." "They are too expensive." "Why spend money on something that won't look good on me?"

As I dig a bit deeper, the real issues start to surface: "I don't deserve to wear nice clothes when I am fat". "If I look good I may not have the incentive to lose weight." So what you are telling yourself is that when you are fat you have no self-confidence and self-esteem, so you play out the part, right down to the dull dreary dress. The messages we give ourselves subconsciously are very strong.

It is time now to do some shedding of your wardrobe. I want you to go through your wardrobe and sort your clothes into: never wear, sometimes wear, frequently wear. Get rid of the clothes you don't like or never wear; give them away or store them. Your wardrobe should only contain clothes that you like, that fit you well and that look flattering. If you do this exercise seriously, your wardrobe should be at least halved. Be ruthless. It might mean going shopping again and getting new clothes.

If you don't discard your thin wardrobe, ask yourself: "Would I really get full use of these clothes if I were to fit in them again? Would these clothes be too dated?" Keeping your thin wardrobe could set you up to strive for unrealistic goals. We are living in the present, not the past, nor the future.

Dieter's belief: Never buy a size larger. At all costs, try to fit into the smaller size. It gives more incentive to lose weight.

The other day I was in a clothes shop and a woman was trying desperately to fit into a size 12 skirt. The shop assistant was trying to be polite and told her the size 14 would be more flattering. The young girl looked at her, horrified, and said, "I am never going to wear a size 14; I will get into this if it kills me!" And it probably will. She will take the garment home, realise how ridiculous it looks, throw it in the back of her wardrobe and vow to go on a crash diet until she can fit into it. Why? Because a size 14 means 'fat', it means being beaten, giving into fat and accepting her real size.

We place far too much emphasis on clothes sizes. In the

woman's mind a size 14 was a gigantic leap from a 12, but in reality it is hardly the case. A friend of mine in the rag trade has told me that sizes are so different and vary so much from garment to garment, and label to label, that you should never pay attention to them. The sizes in my wardrobe vary from a size 10 to 16.

One popular clothing label has even changed their sizing structure so that a 12 is now a 10. Manufacturers are not silly. They will prey on your desire to be that bit slimmer, even if it is by illusion. How many times have you tried on a garment in your normal dress size and it was loose and you felt really good about it because you believed you had lost weight? Some of the mirrors just don't seem to be quite right either, do they? Marilyn Monroe was a size 14 to 16, and men still go 'gaga' over her. Men will think a particular woman is sexy, curvy and voluptuous, whereas women will say that she is too fat. We place unrealistic expectations on ourselves and are far too critical of other women.

HANDY HINTS

CUT OFF ALL SIZE LABELS.
BUY FOR COMFORT, LOOK AND FIT, NOT SIZE.
YOU ARE NOT GIVING IN BY ACCEPTING YOUR SIZE, YOU ARE TAKING CARE OF YOURSELF
BY LIVING IN THE PRESENT.

CHAPTER TWENTY-FIVE

BODY MOVEMENT —
THE NEW APPROACH TO EXERCISE

Dieter's belief: Exercise is boring hard work and the only way to lose weight. I must punish myself by doing more if I eat too much.

Most of us with weight issues usually fall into two categories when it comes to exercise: 'do it under sufferance' or 'forget it'. Category two seems to be the most popular. Most of us are burnt out, sick and tired of the diet and exercise treadmill. We can all tell stories about humiliation when exercising. My whole exercising period when dieting was one big humiliation. I used to go to aerobics classes diligently when I was dieting, and there was always the size 8, gym 'sexpot', with the tiny leotard including g-string up her bum, right in front of me. My mind was never on the exercises I was supposed to be doing; it was always questioning why I didn't have her figure. Why wasn't I born with skinny legs? Why can't my boobs be small or like hers? Why? Why? Why? So I would walk out of the gym feeling ten times more miserable than when I went in. I would then go home, straight to the kitchen, and eat. I'm sure you can all relate to similar stories.

My exercise routine would only coincide with a diet routine. The minute I was off the diet, exercise went out the window. It was also quite physically impossible for me to exercise because I was too full from eating.

Once you get off the treadmill of dieting and into self-empowerment you will find that you have a completely different outlook on life, including exercise. Replace the harmful belief that exercise is torture with the belief that body movement is fun.

Do you exercise for fun? Remember the fun you had as a child — relay races, hopscotch, hide-and-seek. Did you ever think of burning calories or reducing fat? No. You were out for 100 per cent pure fun. What happened with your thoughts on exercise as you grew older? Maybe you were punished by over-enthusiastic parents who saw you as an Olympic gold medalist who was not allowed to get on with life until you finished your laps? Or maybe you have embarrassing memories of failing at exercise? Whatever happened in the past, leave it there. Look now to the future and start to see exercise in a different light. I like the expression 'body movement'. It sounds more caring and less militant than 'exercise'. The truth is that if you do exercise, you do burn up more calories and raise your metabolism. That is a scientific fact. But why bust your guts doing something you hate and for all the wrong reasons?

I bet if I were to look in your garage or storeroom, I would find hidden in a corner somewhere an exercise bike, or treadmill, or gutbuster, or some type of exercise equipment — no doubt bought with good intentions, lured by the model demonstrating it. But let's be realistic: How exciting is a walking machine or exercise bike? The novelty wears off at an alarming rate. A friend of mine buys every new machine that comes on the market. She says she doesn't have time to exercise and hops on one of her latest gadgets. But then I see her out walking. "Can't beat fresh air", she says with a laugh.

Get to know your capabilities, likes and dislikes
Are you a morning person who jumps out of bed at the crack of

BODY MOVEMENT — THE NEW APPROACH TO EXERCISE

dawn? Do you like to go for a brisk walk in the morning, or would you prefer to stay curled up in bed? At what time of day would you prefer to do some sort of physical activity? Expand your thinking about body movement. It doesn't have to be sweating it out in the gym or running along the road. If you are doing some sort of exercise as a form of punishment, chances are your rate of injury will be high, as your body and mind are resisting what you are doing. I discovered I love walking through the botanical gardens, dancing around my lounge room, and yoga. Choose a form of body movement that will enhance your self-esteem and well-being, not destroy it.

HANDY HINTS

START SOME GENTLE BODY MOVEMENT THAT MAKES YOU FEEL GOOD INSIDE AND OUT.

DEEP BREATHING IS AN ESSENTIAL PART OF YOUR HEALTH, FOR BODY, MIND AND SPIRIT.

CHAPTER TWENTY-SIX

HOW TO RAPIDLY
INCREASE YOUR SELF-ESTEEM

Dieter's belief: My self-image will only improve when I lose weight.

Self-esteem does not result from how thin, smart, attractive, successful or popular you are. Just look at how miserable the lives of some famous movie stars and models are, and it is not hard to realise that external things have nothing to do with self-esteem. Before you can increase your self-esteem, you must learn to look honestly and openly at how you have been treating yourself and resolve to confront the dislike you have for your body. Be honest, confront the obvious. The negative thoughts you have about your body have only led to misery, self-hate, depression and anger. You also need to recognise that the notion of 'thin means beautiful' is dangerous because if you believe it, it implies to you that being fat is ugly, no good, revolting, etc. Self-acceptance is the first stepping stone to peace of mind.

Self-esteem usually hits rock bottom when eating out of control is at an all time high. All of us suffer some degree of low self-esteem from time to time, but when we have a weight problem we suffer most of the time. Feeling fat hits right to the core of our self-esteem. When we go out in public, all we can think about is how fat we look compared to everyone else. It consumes us, obsesses us and sends us very quickly down our spiral of despair. We say to ourselves: "I am too fat to have any self-esteem, how can I possibly feel good when I look like this? When I get thin my self-esteem will increase." What we are telling ourselves is: stay fat and stay depressed. How can we ever change with this state of mind?

When we are thin we feel that we are acceptable to the outside world. The more pretty we look on the outside, the more comments we get like this: "Hey, you look great! You have lost weight and look so healthy and young." When we diet to gain acceptance, we are buying into the system that says we are not acceptable the way we are and that part of us is bad. Eventually we gain the weight back in the hope that someday, someone will tell us we are great and lovable just the way we are. When we are too pre-occupied with diets and our weight, our self-esteem then centres around how good, how bad or how fat/thin we are. And 'bad' and 'fat' mean low self-esteem. We need to unhook the concepts of 'fat' and 'food' from our self-esteem by learning to empower ourselves again and changing our dieter's beliefs into empowering beliefs. Most of us latched onto the 'diet/weight' concept to improve our self-esteem, but it did exactly the opposite for us.

Our past influences
Low self-esteem is caused by a variety of factors. We mask it as our weight, but it goes deeper. Parents, peers, school, work relationships and cultural roles — all have, or had, an influence on our self-esteem. It would be ideal if self-acceptance began at home when we were little and so impressionable but, unfortunately, our mothers, and their mothers, suffered the same type of self-hate and conditional external acceptance.

Our background and early childhood experiences determine a lot about the way we perceive our bodies. If you were called 'little, fat dumpling' or 'rolly polly', chances are that you still think you resemble those names. If you were given food for comfort, chances are that you still do this for yourself as an adult.

HOW TO RAPIDLY INCREASE YOUR SELF-ESTEEM

Childhood messages and habits stick deep; they stay with us for a long time. Most of them hold no truth now and need to be discarded, because we are adults and not children any more. The rules have changed. I remember playing Truth and Dare at primary school and I was called the ugliest girl in Grade 6. That stuck with me for much of my adult life, until I was 30. I then realised how ridiculous and harmful this statement was, for the ugly duckling had turned into a beautiful swan long ago.

Who has had an influence on the way you feel about your body? What names have you been called? How have these names affected you? Has this been positive or negative? Do you surround yourself with these people?

Our self-esteem affects nearly everything we say or do; it influences who we choose as friends and lovers, how others treat us and our ability to change. Self-esteem has a lot to do with how capable we feel to live well and enjoy life. Why is it that many of us are so capable, yet we feel like losers, our achievements seem empty? We think failure must be around the corner, even when things are going really well. It is as if we feel we do not deserve any success, and the wrath of God is going to strike us down, because we were too successful this week. This lack of self-esteem makes us crave acceptance, and the easiest way we know how to get acceptance is to get it through materialistic things such as thinness, beauty, career, clothes, household items — all external things. The fact is that it must come from the inside, not the outside. These other worlds are too fragile and when they crash, so does our false self-esteem.

Eight success steps to increase self esteem
1. Self-confidence must start right here and now
Building self-confidence must start right here and now. If you tell yourself that your self-esteem will rise when you get thin, you are living in the future world of fantasy, which is unrealistic. You are telling yourself that all issues and problems will disappear when you get thin. To your subconscious mind it is all just a pipe dream. You can keep dreaming and do nothing about it; that way you

will stay exactly the way you are. Start now! Walk to the mirror with a feeling of inner power and self-confidence. Notice the difference.

2. Do what feels right for you

Do what feels right, that is best for you, not for others. This can be done in an unselfish way. Think about it: Is it better to make a decision that keeps everyone else happy, or that rocks a few boats in the beginning and feels great in the long run? When we lack self-confidence, we have few choices — to flap around in a state of indecision and take no action, to act according to what others expect of us, or to develop self-confidence and do what is right for us.

Most of us make decisions based on what others think. This not only makes us feel defeated, it just adds to the problem of our low self-esteem. We worry so much what other people think or might say, especially we women, for we are taught not to rock the boat or be selfish, that family comes first. Backing out of Lucy's tupperware party may plague us with guilt for the next two months. We are so worried that we may have offended someone.

You will only end up stressed, sick and miserable this way. You can't please everyone, so don't try. Start pleasing yourself and watch your self-esteem rise. Of course you need to work this in with your life, for there will be some situations when you choose to do things for other people. Find the balance between caring for others and caring for yourself. Start with little things, such as saying you want to spend five minutes a day on your own, and build up from there.

3. Stop focusing on your weight

To make any changes to your eating and your weight, you need to start focusing on self-acceptance. What you focus on you get. After all, lack of self-acceptance and your negative body thoughts account for much of your overeating. When you lose weight as a by-product of self-acceptance and start eating for physical hunger, your weight loss comes with no strings attached. The day someone says, "Hey, you look great!" you won't immediately think they only like you when you are thin. Instead, you will think, "Yes I'm losing weight but, more importantly, I am gaining self-love and happiness."

4. Learn to say 'NO'
Exercise:
Finish the following statements by choosing the most appropriate word from the list provided.

Your list to choose from for questions (a) and (b): spouse, lover, relative, friend, employer, parent, child, strangers, sales assistants, doctors/professional staff, office workers, younger people, older people, men, women, people from different nationalities.
(a) I am most assertive with ...
(b) I am least assertive with ...

Your list to choose from for questions (c) and (d): hugs and kisses, attention, money, job, praise, recognition, my rights, time for myself.
(c) I am least assertive when asking for ...
(d) I am most assertive when asking for ...

Your list to choose from for questions (e) and (f): sexuality, love, anger, other feelings.
(e) I am most assertive when expressing ...
(f) I am least assertive when expressing ...

Is it easier to be assertive with people you don't know or people close to you? Why?

You only get what you want if you ask for it. Even if you do not get what you ask for, you won't know whether you could have had it unless you ask. I am often surprised when people respond to my requests with a 'yes', even though sometimes I feel they could knock me down with a feather. Ask the question or you will never know! Practise saying 'no' to small things first; for example, by not cooking a dinner or not doing ironing. Stand back and watch for any emotional outbursts. Observe your own feelings and take note if you give in, and why. Try. The more you practice being true to yourself, the easier it gets. You must like yourself enough to not worry about other people's disapproval.

A few years ago a friend of mine threw a huge bomb on her family when she said she would not be joining them for Christmas. Jane said that she wanted to spend Christmas on her own. She told me: "I stood back and let all the verbal abuse and emotional blackmail fly past. I was tempted at times to give in to keep the peace. But I stood my ground and told them that just because I do things that they might not like, it doesn't mean I love them any less." That is important for people to know, for many will take things personally. More important is that you don't go off on a big guilt trip because you were assertive. Being assertive is about making a decision you feel right about and sticking to your guns. Explain your situation in a loving way, and enjoy the outcome of being true to yourself.

I used to have real difficulty with hearing the word 'no', so I decided to challenge my biggest fear and do some door-to-door selling. I went to an unfamiliar town and doorknocked. I was rejected most of the time. I have since taken up learning selling skills. I cringed every time I tried to sell and it was really difficult to hear the word 'no'. I would be waiting for it, all tensed up. Then I started to ask myself why hearing 'no' was so bad anyway. After all, it was not me personally they were saying 'no' to, it was the product. I started accepting that hearing the word 'no' was part of everyday life. While sitting in the park with Kev after my week of selling, Kev turned to me and said, jokingly, "Oh well, there's $17 for the week — well done!" I had to see the funny side and just rolled on the grass laughing, just happy to still have my sense of humour — luckily for Kev, too.

5. The best way to get what you want is to ask for it
Children do this all the time; they do not beat around the bush. The other day my friend Suzie turned to me and said, "Di, what are you doing at 8.00 tomorrow morning?" "Why?" I asked. "Well, I was just wondering, if you weren't doing anything, maybe, if you aren't busy, that is, if it's not out of your way ..." "Yes?" I said, expecting some huge request.

"Suzie," I finally said, "just try to tell me directly and in one sentence what you want. Whichever way you ask, the answer will be 'yes' or 'no'". All Suzie had wanted was a lift to work, but she had a great deal of difficulty asking for the favour. She was brought up in a family that never wanted to inconvenience friends by asking favours. But the direct approach is less painful, and you will get your question over and done with a lot quicker. By the way, Suzie is doing much better at making her requests now with the more direct approach.

6. You don't have to be perfect

Are you a perfectionist? Did you know that perfectionists do not like themselves very much? Did you know that perfectionists see things from a negative viewpoint, and end up very unhappy people? Being a perfectionist means that your life will never be quite right; you will never be satisfied with who you are and what you have achieved, no matter how great. It means you are a self-critic. You have a mind-set of 'no good until', but that 'until' never comes. Aiming for perfection may sound good, but in reality it is looking for fault. How many times have you been praised for doing something, only to say or think, "yes, but it could have been better"? Perfectionism serves no purpose except to keep us unhappy.

Perfectionism is difficult to give up — after all, it is your means of survival and coping. The worse you feel, the more of a perfectionist you become. It gives you a reason for your self-hate. Perfectionism keeps you in the fairyland of hope: "When I do this or when I get that, then I will be happy". "When I am slim, I will be happy." Perfectionism protects you from the fear of "I can't stay this good. If nothing is ever good enough, I don't have to worry about living up to the last great performance."

The key is to keep your goals small and achievable and give yourself credit for them. Look for the good within you, instead of looking for perfection, which is fault-finding. Perfectionists are very unforgiving of themselves and others. Stop blaming yourself and others and, once again, check out your belief systems.

7. Be aware of your judgments and jealousy

Jealousy and judgments make our self-esteem plummet. How lousy do you feel when you judge others and get jealous? I remember many times walking into a room and sizing up my competition in the beauty and thin stakes. It is a very, very painful way to live, and it is a 'no-win' situation. There will always be someone thinner, someone younger or someone more attractive than you. Judgments serve no purpose except to make you feel inadequate. We only judge others because we have been judged. We judge others as we judge ourselves. How harshly you judge others is how harshly you judge yourself; after all, other people are mirrors of ourselves. Accept what fine qualities you have and keep reinforcing them to yourself every day, day after day after day. Repetition of a self-love affirmation coupled with a true feeling of wanting to like yourself will win out, and one day you will accept and like who you are.

Next time you go to a shopping centre, observe how much time you spend judging others. It will shock you. How much of your day is spent judging others? Their dress, their weight, their face and clothing? Do you find that when you are feeling self-critical, you judge others more? Catch yourself judging and stamp it out. Whenever you start thinking you want to be as thin as someone you see, counteract the judgment with a neutral statement like, 'the grass is green'. This will make the judgment seem a lot less important. It puts things back into perspective. I do not think you can ever stop judging, but you can become more aware of doing it and distance yourself from it. Judgments do not lead to change, but awareness does. Judgments serve no purpose except to make you feel inadequate.

8. A sure way to self-esteem is to be around positive, caring people

You can love yourself as much as you want, but if you go home to a negative, uncaring environment, all your new beliefs will soon be squashed. We all want to be liked, but sometimes we try too hard to be liked. We try to fit in, and this means staying slim, staying young and pretty, saying and doing the right thing. But at what emotional cost? Are you afraid that you may annoy or offend someone if you say how you really feel? Are you so scared that they may come back at you with a comment about your weight? Is that so bad? Make a commitment to yourself that you will be true to your inner feelings and mingle only with positive and caring people who support your growth. Avoid loud, aggressive and negative people, who will only stifle your growth.

So there are the eight steps to building high self-esteem. They are really very simple and straightforward, but very powerful. Even by trying one or two steps, you will be amazed how dramatically your self-esteem will rise. The key is to keep going, as it only gets easier once you push through the initial barrier.

HANDY HINTS

THE BEST WAY TO GET WHAT YOU WANT IS TO ASK FOR IT.

START SAYING 'NO' TO SMALL THINGS, AND BUILD UP FROM THERE.

STATE YOUR OPINION IF YOU DON'T AGREE WITH SOMEONE, RATHER THAN KEEP QUIET.

PART SEVEN

HOW TO TRAVEL
THE HIGHWAY TO SUCCESS

CHAPTER TWENTY-SEVEN

PLANNING
GUARANTEES SUCCESS

No changes ever go exactly according to plan. That is why it is so important to have a back-up plan ready to put into place. People, situations and even ourselves can upset our best laid plans, so we need to be ready for setbacks and quickly knock them on the head. You are probably aware of certain situations or people that are more likely to cause you to have a setback. Setbacks are inevitable. Expect them and you will not be so devastated when they happen, especially if you have a plan of attack. I cannot stress enough how important it is to get out of setbacks quickly, to avoid falling down the spiral of despair.

Remember that setbacks are a part of life and they are a great learning tool. You have been given a goldmine of techniques throughout this book to help you. Having a setback is part of the journey. Just because you have a setback doesn't mean all your efforts have gone down the drain. You are still progressing. You just need to get back on track. You haven't gone back to square one. When I began my journey, my early 'off-track episodes' seemed like a real disaster. I would wallow in self-pity after a binge, thinking that I was useless, that I couldn't stick to anything and that I was doomed to stay fat.

What I was doing was basing my performance on past experiences, just like my failed diets. I gradually learnt, after a few off-the-track episodes, that this was part of life. Not feeling so stressed out about it, I was then able to do something constructive, such as journal writing, to help me understand more about myself. My setback would not seem so bad and I would get back on track a lot more quickly than before. I knew the old way of berating myself had never helped me at all.

Dealing with your high risk situations

Discover your high risk situations and learn skills to help you deal with them. When identified, you can choose the best solution: to avoid, change, or deal better with problems.

Write down some of your trigger situations and your plan of attack. Here are a few examples of my own:

Triggers	Plan of attack
Eating out	Take edge off hunger with a banana
Setting my goals too high	Reward for small gains; re-do goal list
Feeling guilty after bingeing	Learn from binge; take time out to spoil myself; have a bath; re-read notes on bingeing
Feeling tired	Deep breathing exercises; high energy food, if needed

Creating balance in your life

Would you say that you lead a balanced lifestyle? Far from it, is the answer I hear most frequently. I am sure you could come up with many reasons why you don't lead a balanced lifestyle, but they are all excuses. Underlying them is the truth that you don't consider yourself a high enough priority for doing things for yourself. Unless you start to bring more balance into your life, your way of coping will be, once again, reaching for food.

PLANNING GUARANTEES SUCCESS

A balanced lifestyle is one that has a relative degree of balance between those things you must do and things you want to do. An unbalanced lifestyle is characterised by too many 'shoulds' and not enough 'wants'. "I should go shopping", "I should do the washing before I sit down" — the list goes on and on. You only need to look at the large number of advertisements for women low on energy, with offers ranging from more iron, to holidays to exotic herbs. The real answer is inexpensive and simple: put some joy into your life. If your life is filled with more work than play, more obligations than rewards, it takes your energy and directs it outward, with little or no time or energy left for activities that give personal pleasure, satisfaction or self-fulfillment. This leads to feelings of deprivation and wanting, to a need for self-indulgence, and then the setback risk is very high. If you are not getting very much joy out of the things you do in life, you will keep turning to food to give you some of the pleasures you feel are missing.

Exercise:
Create a chart like the one below to give you insights into your situation.

Activity	Want to	Have to	Satisfaction
Paid Work		✓	M
Yoga	✓		H

Key: High = H Medium = M Low= L

Have a good look at your list. Of your 'have tos', how many of them rated high or medium on the satisfaction level? How many rated low? How much of your day is spent on 'have tos' and at what level of satisfaction? If many of your 'have tos' were low on satisfaction, you need to reassess what it is you are doing and add more 'want tos' in your life.

Things I love to do or would like to now start doing
If you found your list rather depressing, start to bring more fun

things into your life. Begin by creating another chart and filling it in with activities you would like to do more of.

Activity	Cost	Who with	How often	Priority
Movies	$10.00	Friend	Once per f/night	High
Yoga	Nil	Self	Daily	High

Rank your preferences from one to ten. Nurture yourself and do an activity once a week.

Creating a daily routine

Routines are easy to do and easy not to do. Your inner happiness and progression will depend on your doing your daily routine on a regular basis — this means every day. A daily routine is necessary if you want to live in tune with your natural body cycles.

Try to rise when you wake up. If you do, you will feel energetic and light. We all know that groggy feeling if we oversleep (however, as heads of households I don't think many of us experience that feeling too often!). As soon as you open your eyes, think positive thoughts about your life now and how you visualise it will become. Have an attitude of gratitude for all the things you have in life. Do a few stretches in bed and then a few out of bed. Do a few minutes of deep breathing and take a brisk walk around the neighbourhood or devote a few minutes to your favourite body movement.

Before you shower, dry skin massage your body with a bristle brush. This will stimulate circulation and help your body get rid of toxins. A light rubbing of aromatherapy oils after your shower is also great. They rejuvenate and revitalise your mental and physical being.

While you are in the bathroom, look into the mirror and say, "I love you", and mean it! You might feel silly in the beginning, but this is just an indication of how much you really don't love yourself. Please persevere until you believe it! Looking yourself in the eye with positive affirmations is very powerful — you are talking directly to your soul.

PLANNING GUARANTEES SUCCESS

As the day draws to a close, get in touch with the beauty of nature around you. Watch the sun set, walk barefoot in your garden or along a beach, watch the surf or take a dip if you dare. Try going to bed around 10.00 pm. This is nature's slow cycle and if you stay up later, you may have more difficulty sleeping or have a restless sleep. And lastly, just before you drop off to sleep, be grateful for the good things in your day and visualise how you want your life to be. Let your last thoughts be of peace and happiness. If you are on severe time constraints, just cut down on the time you take to do these things. It is vital that you do something every day to assist in the development of your new lifestyle, for this registers in your mind that change is consistent and therefore ongoing. If you do a bit of 'this and that' a few days a week, your mind registers that it is only a half-hearted effort, and you will never get ahead. I cannot stress this enough: just five minutes a day will make a big difference. Otherwise, before you know it, you will be digging into the cookie jar.

HANDY HINTS

CONSTANTLY RE-AFFIRM THAT SETBACKS ARE A LEARNING TOOL.
CREATE A BALANCE OF 'WANT TO' AND 'HAVE TO' IN YOUR LIFE.
STICK TO AND ENJOY A SIMPLE, DAILY ROUTINE.

CHAPTER TWENTY-EIGHT
PUTTING IT ALL TOGETHER

Eating and Food

As we approach the end of the book it is important to recap the major points and put them into a workable daily routine for yourself. I have listed below, the different areas of change and what to do on a daily basis. Once you incorporate these strategies into your daily life they will become second nature very quickly. So lets begin with eating.

Before you begin eating a meal, assess your hunger level and do a check. Close your eyes, and visualise at what scale your hunger is on, what type of food your body wants to eat, including the texture and temperature. As you eat, prepare the food as nicely as can be. Sit down without distractions and enjoy your food, really focusing on the texture, taste, smell, and look of the food. Be aware of how the food makes you feel, emotionally and physically. Pay close attention to your "I'm full" signals, and try your best to leave the table or to stop eating when you still feel good about yourself. If you feel you have eaten past your satisfaction and comfort level, comfort yourself and understand that it may take some time, after all those dieting years or deprivation, to get in touch with your normal eating style. After you have eaten, allow 1 minute to let the food go down, and focus on your feelings. Follow the same awareness process when you next decide to eat.

If you eat when not physically hungry, that is OK. Don't give yourself a hard time. Try to find out what is bothering you, do some deep breathing and see if any other feelings surface that depend on food to be buried again. Try to let them surface a little longer before you decide to eat, and see if you can pinpoint familiar situations or feelings that turn you to food. Pay close attention to the type of food you eat and how you are feeling as you eat it and after you finish. After you have eaten, do some journal writing or talk aloud to the food. Make sure you do something extra nice for yourself. You are probably needing comfort.

Other daily exercises
As you go about your daily work and incorporate your new eating guidelines into your life, choose to work on one other aspect that is not directly related to food. Work with it for a day, a week or more, till you feel comfortable that you understand or that it is working for you. Then move onto another exercise. Remember always to do one thing a day, no matter how small or insignificant it may seem, as you are registering to your subconscious mind that change is happening on a regular basis. Doing one thing for an hour or so one day a week is ineffective, as it doesn't register long-term and continual change to your mind. This is vitally important for you to understand. Choose one or more of the following exercises in the area you feel a need to work on.

As a guide, 5–10 mins a day is a minimum time for your growth work.

Mind work
affirmations
visualisations
role absorption

PUTTING IT ALL TOGETHER

journal writing
mirror work
new belief writing

Eating
eating guidelines
hunger and satisfaction
true and lure food checks

Body Work
wardrobe shredding
buying clothes that look and feel good
enjoyable body movement
learn more about how your body works

Emotional work
write about or draw your emotions
do some journal writing
deep breathe as soon as you feel uncomfortable emotions arising

Life Savers
deep breathing meeting and bringing your 'inner carer' into your daily life.

HANDY HINTS
CREATE AN EASY TO ACHIEVE AND FOLLOW, DAILY ROUTINE FOR YOURSELF.
WRITE YOUR ROUTINE ON A BUSINESS SIZE CARD AND KEEP IT IN YOUR WALLET AS A REMINDER.

CHAPTER TWENTY-NINE

QUESTIONS AND ANSWERS

You may have some questions you would like answered. Here are the questions which I am asked most frequently and their answers. I'm sure they will assist you in some way.

QUESTION: Can I do this on my own?
ANSWER: Yes, as with anything in your life, no matter how much help and encouragement you are given, the end result is up to you! You have all the necessary skills within you and this book will guide you and give you encouragement when you need it. Joining self-help groups and being around positive people is also vitally important for your success. Keeping a journal, too, is a wonderful tool for self-help and learning about yourself. Getting it down on paper is very powerful; it gets it out of your head space; it then stares you in the face. I also strongly recommend that you work with a trained therapist to overcome some of your deeply embedded harmful belief structures.

QUESTION: How can I manage with little support by those in my household?
ANSWER: The beauty of this program is that you are not doing anything to alienate yourself from your family. In fact you are doing the exact opposite: learning to fit in again with your eating and become a so-called 'normal eater' again. The less you draw attention to yourself, the less people will worry about what is on your plate or what dress size you are.

QUESTION: What happens if I fall back into diet mode?
ANSWER: You have been given many rescue strategies throughout the book to help you with this one. If you do find yourself slipping again, it's time for some journal writing. View the situation without emotion and see how dieting has not helped you at all and that it is a no-win situation. Don't be too hard on yourself, but persevere. This is the only path to happiness.

QUESTION: How can I really convince myself that I can lose weight?
ANSWER: By trusting and working with your Inner Wisdom and remembering that your body is wanting to help you get back to an ideal weight that is right for you. Don't focus on failed diets — that will hinder your progress. Just look forward and keep trusting and have faith in your wisdom, which wants to help, not hinder, your progress.

QUESTION: Won't I put some equally destructive habit in the place of my food?
ANSWER: You will only do this if you are unaware of the root cause of your conflicts with food. If you don't explore the root of your eating problem, you will hop from one bad habit to another. These habits then become compulsive behaviours, which lock out the other thoughts and prevent you from looking deeply into yourself. As soon as painful emotions surface, don't block them out by turning to food. Although this may seem a lot easier than looking deeply into yourself, it will only hinder your progress. The rewards of awareness and self-growth are too good to be put

QUESTIONS AND ANSWERS

into words. All areas of your life become fantastic — personal power, self-esteem, self-love are but a few. If you have a compulsive tendency, I strongly suggest you seek the help of an experienced, honest and loving therapist.

QUESTION: You say to eat what I want, but I have dietary restrictions due to my health.
ANSWER: A lot of people have special dietary requirements. Taking care of yourself is the most important thing. Start looking at your illness from a holistic viewpoint and look to see what emotions are giving you pain, for they play a large part in your physical health problems. Work as broadly as you can within your dietary constraints. Try working on other areas of your life rather than just your food.

QUESTION: Eating without distractions is virtually impossible for me. What do you suggest?
ANSWER: Nothing is impossible; some things require effort. You choose every action in your life, so don't ever blame situations or other people. How important is eating to you? When you eat, eat; when you read, read. The purpose of the eating steps is to heighten your enjoyment of food and to help you stay aware of each aspect of the eating experience, which you have buried a long time ago. If, after experimenting, you find you can read and still be aware and enjoy eating, so be it. The eating steps are just guidelines to help you get in touch with yourself again.

CHAPTER THIRTY

WHERE TO FROM HERE?

There is no end to a rainbow
Well, my dear friends, here we are at the end — of the book, anyway. Your mind is probably racing, trying to digest all this new information, and you may be wondering how you are going to do it all. The key, as I have said all along, is to take small steps, at a steady pace, at which you feel comfortable. Give yourself at least one year to implement your success steps, although you will start to see changes immediately.

Now is the time to put all this information into practise. Re-read this book and master the techniques and principles. Don't just read this book and put it down, saying, "Oh, that was very interesting". Get on with the job! Only you can do it. No one else can do it for you.

Keep the process of growth going. You have no option but to bring yourself back to self-empowerment if you want to lose weight and be a happy person. Remember, the more you practice the eating success steps and other techniques in this book, the easier things will become. You will always be tested along the way. Getting back on track gets easier and quicker, and pinpointing trigger situations and emotions gets easier. But you will always be on a constant learning curve — remember to love the plateaus of growth. I encourage you to set up support groups with other women who think the same way: meet socially and allow some time to talk about how things are going.

After three months of following the success steps, check your progress, using the following chart. This will enable you to see where you might need some help and where things are going well for you:

ACTION	YES	NEEDS MORE WORK
Eating		
I have stopped counting calories		
I have stopped weighing myself		
I eat when I am hungry		

ACTION	YES	NEEDS MORE WORK
I can stop eating when I am satisfied		
I eat in full view of people		
I have legalised *all* foods		
I accept my body		
I give 15 minutes a day to myself		
I eat sitting down in a pleasant environment		
I have an abundance of food around me		
Body		
I accept my body		
I dress to look and feel good		
I do regular exercise for mind, body and soul		
Emotions		
I am able to express my emotions		
I praise myself		
I can say 'no'		
I am more conscious of all that I do		
I don't give myself a hard time when I have a setback		
I treat myself with kindness and compassion		

WHERE TO FROM HERE?

Other areas I need to spend more time on are …
My priority area is …
What I need to put into action straight away for my priority area is …

What are the areas not working for you? Check the areas where there is the most frustration. Remember, identifying the problem is ninety per cent of the solution. Persevere with your newfound self-discipline and you shall reap the rewards of your effort. The first actions must start within your mind. Turn your beliefs around and your life will change. Persistence, faith and confidence will take you through all the walls of self-doubt, and you will be greatly rewarded. Give yourself at least one year to successfully come back to your natural eating cycle. Do not diet again and, most importantly, enjoy every day of your life!

Thank you for sharing this journey with me throughout these pages. I will always be here in these pages to give you help, encouragement and guidance. I will not wish you luck — that is hoping by chance. *You* know that positive action will take you towards your goals. Your rewards will far exceed your expectations.

I wish you every success.

BIBLIOGRAPHY AND
FURTHER READING

Emotions

Hay, Louise. *You Can Heal Your Life*, (Concord, NSW: Specialist Publications, 1984).

Lerner, Harriet. G., Ph.D. *The Dance of Anger*, (New York: Harper & Row, 1985).

Rowland, Michael. *Absolute Happiness*, (Bondi Beach, NSW: Self Communications, 1993).

Roth, Geneen. *When Food is Love*, (New York: Penguin Group, 1992).

Stone, Hal, Ph.D. and Stone, Sidra, Ph.D. *Embracing Ourselves*, (Mill Valley, CA: Nataraj Publishing, 1989).

Stone, Sidra, Ph.D. *The Shadow King*, (Mill Valley, CA: Nataraj Publishing, 1987).

Stone, Hal and Stone, Sidra. *Embracing your Inner Critic*, (Mill Valley, CA: Delos Inc, 1993).

Body work

Cooke, Kaz. *Real Gorgeous*, (St Leonards, NSW: Allen & Unwin, 1994).

Dytchwald, Ken. *Body Mind*, (New York: Pantheon Books, 1977).

Harrison, Dr John. *Love Your Disease–it's Keeping You Healthy*, (North Ryde, NSW: Angus & Robertson, 1984).

Hay, Louise L. *Love Your Body*, (Concord, NSW: Specialist Publications, 1990).
Hirschmann, Jane R. and Munter, Carol H. *When Women Stop Hating Their Bodies*, (United States: Ballantine Books, 1995).
Leonard, George and Murphy, Michael. *The Life We Are Given*, (New York: Penguin Putnam Inc, 1995).
Northrup, Dr Christiane. *Women's Body, Women's Wisdom*, (London: Judy Piatkus Publishers, 1995).

Eating
Chopra, Deepak. *Perfect Weight*, (London: Rider, 1994).
Hirschmann, Jane and Munter, Carol. *Overcoming Overeating*, (USA: Ballantine Books, 1990).
Kratina, Karin, MA, RD, LD; King, Nancy L., MS, RD, CDE and Hayes, Dayle, MS, RD, LD. *Moving Away From Diets*, (Lake Dallas: Helm Seminars, 1996).
Kano, Susan. *Making Peace with Food*, (USA Haper Perinial, 1989).
Orbach, Suzie. Fat is a Feminist Issue II, (New York: Berkley Books, 1982).
Roth, Geneen. *Breaking Free from Compulsive Eating*, (New York: Penguin, 1986).
Why Weight? A Guide to Ending Compulsive Eating, (New York: Penguin Group, 1989).
Ribole, Evelyn, and MS.R.D. and Resch, Elyse, MS.R.D. *Intuitive Eating*, (New York: St Marin's Press, 1995).

Women's Issues
Hutchinson, Marcia Germaine. *Transforming Body Image*, (USA: Marcia Germaine Hutchinson, 1985).
Friday, Nancy. *My Mother, Myself*, (USA: Delacorte Press, 1977).
Louden, Jennifer. *The Women's Comfort Book*, (New York: Harper Collins, 1992).
Woolger, Jennifer Barker and Woolger, Roger J. *The Goodness Within*, (London: Random Century Group, 1990).
Healthy Weight Journal (USA) – Decker Publishing

DI HARRIS SEMINARS AND COURSES

If you would like to receive further information or attend any of Di Harris's seminars, please send your details on the form below or on a photocopied page.

Di conducts several courses and there are cassette tapes available which expand further on the information you have read in this book. They are packed full of inspiring and powerful information and techniques, presented in a dynamic, fun, non-threatening way.

It is a great experience to be with Di in person. If you would like to attend any of her presentations or receive a catalogue of what is available, then phone or write to:

Di Harris Seminars
PO Box 359
Blackheath. NSW 2785
AUSTRALIA
Phone (Toll-free) 1800 112 116

For further Information
POST TO: Di Harris Seminars, PO Box 359 Blackheath
NSW 2785, Australia
ENQUIRIES: (toll-free) 1800 112 116

I would like to find out more information about Di's
❏   workshops   ❏   audio tapes

Please send information to:

Name (first)   (surname)
_____

Address
_____

City   Postcode
_____

Phone (h)   (w)
_____